OVERVIEW

Overview
Effective Interfunctional Relationships
"Great discoveries and achievements invariably involve the cooperation of many minds." - Alexander Graham Bell, inventor of the telephone.

In an organization, it's very easy for one to become isolated in a world mostly composed of the people one works with directly. As demands for efficiency and effectiveness grow in today's competitive marketplace, you'll find that the formation of interfunctional relationships and teams can help you meet this demand.

James
James is the head of design for a development firm, and he has a reputation for being difficult to work with. The truth is that he just prefers to do things by himself.

Amy
Amy is the sales manager for a consulting firm. She encourages her staff to work with people in other departments, and she belongs to several interfunctional teams.

1

Cooperation across functions and departments may run counter to natural instincts, but in today's business environment, it's worth the effort because it's necessary and produces better results.

If you've already been involved with interfunctional relationships in your job, this course offers you the opportunity to learn skills that will help you improve those relationships. In this course, you'll explore:

- negotiating territories in the workplace,
- building interfunctional alliances,
- improving cross-functional communication.

Effective Relationships with Customers

Working effectively with customers can be as impersonal and awkward or as intimate and graceful as dancing with a partner. To dance well, you need to know how your partner moves and you need to know the dance steps. Knowing one but not the other won't get you around the dance floor together. Whether your company deals with individual walk-ins or with vast conglomerates, it profits from customers' extended and repeat business.

Demographics might help you locate and define your market, but ultimately, you have to deal with customers one by one, on an individual basis. And that means getting to know them and building relationships with them.

Working effectively with customers consists of far more than simply returning their calls and showing some courtesy.

A relationship with a customer requires active development, maintenance, and follow-through. And it benefits from a solid, defined commitment.

In this course, you'll learn how to develop and maintain long-term customer relationships by using the necessary elements for working effectively with customers:

- defining your vendor role,
- cultivating customer relationships,
- advancing long-term relationships with customers.

Effective Intercultural Relationships

"It's a small world after all." --Richard Sherman, songwriter

Spanish. Chinese. Canadian. Polynesian. Nigerian. Brazilian. Egyptian.

When was the last time you made it through an entire day without interacting with someone from a different cultural background than yours?

Whether it was at the corner market or in a multinational business; in a small, regional office or a global corporate headquarters; at a local lunch function or on a business trip on the other side of the world; chances are increasingly good that you will be interacting with business personnel who come from a different cultural background than you.

You don't need to look to country borders to notice cultural differences; there are various neighborhood cultural enclaves in most towns these days. Even if you're speaking the same language, you can't assume that you share perspectives.

As the workplace evolves, the need to build effective intercultural relationships becomes more than good practice--it becomes a necessity. The value of building healthy relationships is essential when you consider that:

- the global marketplace is multicultural,

- most businesses are culturally integrated,
- it improves understanding of different perspectives.

This course is designed to build your awareness of the ways in which communication can vary among cultures and to build your skills for communicating more effectively across varying cultural business situations. You will learn how to embrace cultural differences, examine the meaning behind the context, and discover the value of obeying the customs and etiquette of cultures different from your own.

Effective Intergender Relationships

One of the biggest diversity challenges in today's business world is learning how to effectively work with a member of the opposite gender.

Why can't a man be more like a woman? And why can't a woman be more like a man? In the private and social spheres of life, the differences can be fun and celebrated. At work, though, you need to get along with the other gender and communicate equally well with women and men.

Today's rapidly changing business environment makes your intergender communication skills critical to your success.

Women and men are different anatomically, biologically, and socially. Even some of the ways their

brains function are different. But the differences in their intellects and abilities are individual, not gender- related. The difference in how men and women perceive and present themselves is mostly a sociocultural phenomenon, like the differences that arise in people raised in different cultures or countries.

Consider the communication problems of the fictional Tarzan, a British citizen from a prosperous family, brought up by apes in Africa. It was the way Tarzan was raised in the jungle - the socialization differences--that created communication problems, not his abilities or intellect.

If someone speaks Italian and your understanding of Italian is minimal, you're going to miss a lot of the content and nuance. The obvious solution is to learn more Italian. You don't have to unlearn your native language to become fluent in another. Instead, you become bilingual.

Different languages

Often men and women seem to communicate as if they are using different languages.

Improved communication

Understanding the communication differences between the genders provides a basis for better comprehension and improved communication.

The lessons in this course will help you develop an understanding and appreciation for the other gender's communication style. They will also provide you with some skills that can improve your work interactions with members of the opposite gender.

CHAPTER ONE
Effective Interfunctional Relationships

Territorial Instincts at Work

Because the territorial instinct is universal, it operates on everyone in the workplace. It affects the ways that people interact with each other and the ways that they do their jobs. The fact that it affects everyone makes it essential that you understand exactly what territoriality is and how it functions in this environment.

Our remote ancestors defended their cave homes from neighboring tribes and fierce beasts using stones and crude spears. The territorial instinct is as common to humans as it is to nonhuman animals. It's a genetic leftover from Stone Age ancestors who had to physically defend their territory to survive.

Almost anything you can conceive as being personally important can be defined as a defendable territory, even a metaphorical cloud. How people define their territorial boundaries may fluctuate, but one thing doesn't change. In every era, people stake out their territory and defend it avidly against encroachment. Within the confines of the work world, where physical work space fluctuates, there are three primary conceptual territory types that people instinctually stake out and defend.

Encountering problems with territoriality is a common occurrence for many people. It takes a lot of energy to keep from intruding upon the territory other people have staked out in the workplace, and sometimes it's just downright impossible.

How territorial instincts function in the workplace

The final reinforcements were almost in place. A few more shields to block incoming stares and a sign on the stapler, identifying its owner, would complete the job. Larry had finally secured his cubicle as his kingdom.

Does this sound extreme to you? You might laugh, but how many times have you had to track down your stapler or your favorite pen? Human beings are territorial by nature. This territoriality is evident on the grand scale in the existence of national boundaries and the wars that are fought to defend those boundaries. On a much smaller scale, this same territoriality shows up every day in your working environment.

Because the territorial instinct is universal, it operates on everyone in the workplace. It affects the ways that people interact with each other and the ways that they do their jobs. The fact that it affects everyone makes it essential that you understand exactly what territoriality is and how it functions in this environment.

Allowing your territorial instinct to act unchecked at work can negatively affect your desired outcomes. Learning to work around your territorial instinct to build interfunctional relationships can produce better results for you and for your projects.

The value of understanding territoriality in the workplace

Modify the effects

To be able to modify the effects territorial instincts have on your workplace, you must first have an understanding of how they function.

Know yourself

Any understanding you gain of instinctual behavior will add to your own understanding of yourself and the instincts by which you function.

Though you will encounter some amount of territoriality in every work relationship, the need to defend territory becomes especially important when people are working across functions. Nothing will ruin an interfunctional alliance more quickly than ongoing turf wars. In this lesson, you'll explore the basis for turf conflicts, the conceptual territories that exist in the workplace, and the steps for negotiating workplace territory. Territoriality may be instinct, but that doesn't mean you can't still work to gain control of that instinct.

Territorial defense strategies

Our remote ancestors defended their cave homes from neighboring tribes and fierce beasts using stones and crude spears. The territorial instinct is as common to humans as it is to nonhuman animals. It's a genetic leftover from Stone Age ancestors who had to physically defend their territory to survive.

You don't see too many business people hefting rocks from behind their desks. Nevertheless, territoriality continues to thrive under other guises in the workplace.

Although vestigial, the territorial instinct still influences behavior, even when the behavior is counterproductive. Territoriality is rampant in the workplace. In this topic, you'll learn about the different types of defensive behavior that make up the following three territorial defense strategies commonly seen at work:

- personal defense,
- information manipulation,
- placement of communication barriers.

Ignoring, intimidating, and censoring are all common types of personal defense used to defend work territory. When animals bare their teeth, show their claws, or growl, they're employing intimidation. Intimidation relies on attitude: how a message is delivered rather than its content. Ignoring is defense by exclusion or deliberate disregard.

Defensive behaviors
Intimidation

Generally, the higher a person's position in the organization, the more she relies on intimidation as a territorial defense.

Ignoring

Do you know someone who doesn't return calls? Who behaves as if he's too important to notice co-workers? That's defense by ignoring.

Censure is a more aggressive type of personal defense because it involves active disapproval or criticism. The intention is to reduce the perceived credibility of the target. A person exhibiting this defense is merely defending her own work niche against a perceived threat.

As an example of censure, consider Rona's situation. Rona is a project manager for a design firm. She felt threatened by Lance, a newcomer to the department.

Rona saw Lance as a threat to her own advancement. She had a conversation with Travis in which she censured Lance to protect her niche.

Rona: Well, you know how Lance is, Travis. His projects always go over budget. And he hardly ever makes a deadline.

Travis: Really, Rona? I thought Lance was a comer with a lot of potential. Rona: I know the section chief treats Lance like a rising star, but that won't last long.

Travis: Why do you say that?

Rona: He'll run out of ideas to "borrow" soon enough.

Travis: Oh, you mean like that marketing campaign idea he got when he brainstormed with the development group?

Rona: I'd bet that was originally Georgia's idea, not Lance's.

Travis: If that's how Lance works, maybe I'll stay away from that new team he's putting together and stick with your group.

Although defensive behaviors can appear malicious, that's seldom the intention. Rona's territorial instinct drove her to defend her "cave," which in this case was her job niche at work.

The second territorial defense strategy is information manipulation. It's represented by another cluster of three types of defensive behavior: confusion, distraction, and restriction. The goal behind all three types of information manipulation is to maintain control of information that is necessary for co-workers to do their jobs properly. Only the person who controls the information can be productive and look good.

Tactics associated with information manipulation for more information

Confusion

Confusion redirects the perceived competitor's attention to some other matter while the territorial owner strengthens his defenses.

Distraction

Distraction involves excessive focus on a topic with which everyone already agrees. The goal is to clutter a perceived competitor's focus until the territory is safely protected.

Restriction

Restriction refers to hiding, distorting, or refusing access to vital information. The old standby excuse, "The check is in the mail," when it actually isn't, is the classic example of facilitating information manipulation through restriction.

With information manipulation, the information itself serves as the territory that's being defended. It's like the nuts that squirrels bury and hide to feed themselves during the sparse foraging of winter. Squirrels gather nuts instinctively, even when they are in captivity and fed regularly. The outmoded human territorial instinct persists in the same way. In the modern world, pertinent information often determines survival, and workers "squirrel" it away against the threat of a long winter.

The third territorial defense strategy commonly exhibited in the workplace is placement of communication barriers. Controlling access, creating inconvenience, and noncompliance are the associated defensive behaviors. Putting up communication barriers is like building protective walls around your territory. The fewer openings, the easier it is to defend. And you have less need to defend yourself if no one can get to you.

Communication barriers

A gatekeeper

A typical method of controlling access is to establish a secretary or assistant as a gatekeeper with strict orders about who or what gets in or out. Screening phone calls and e-mail serves the same purpose.

Inconvenience

Inconvenience is a communication barrier arranged by generating a complicated schedule for the purpose of limiting access: "Mr. Gray is in a meeting" or "Ms. Brown is out of the office."

Withholding information

A typical noncompliance strategy is withholding or delaying strategic data or information: "Didn't I send you those figures you needed for the meeting? My e-mail server must be malfunctioning."

It's not surprising that it's so difficult to attain true work cooperation. When you look at workplace territorial defense strategies all together, they seem almost comical. But instinctual territorial behavior is a stubborn fact of work life.

The defensive, territorial behavior that appears in co-workers may be conscious or unconscious. It

generally falls into three territorial defense types that all impede the development of cooperative cross-functional relationships:

- personal defense,
- information manipulation,
- placement of communication barriers.
-

Types of workplace territories

"Hey, you, get off of my cloud." - Mick Jagger and Keith Richards

Almost anything you can conceive as being personally important can be defined as a defendable territory, even a metaphorical cloud. How people define their territorial boundaries may fluctuate, but one thing doesn't change. In every era, people stake out their territory and defend it avidly against encroachment. Within the confines of the work world, where physical work space fluctuates, there are three primary conceptual territory types that people instinctually stake out and defend.

Types of workplace territories

Informational territory

In the Information Age, information is the most valuable commodity, often worth more than hard currency. You can trade it, save it, steal it, and invest in it.

Associational territory

Contacts are a source of power. Who you know counts. The more decision-making capacity your contacts have, the more influence you have.

Decisional territory

Decision-making ability is the foundation of all authority. It gives the territory holder power over budget and resource allocations, projects, customers, hiring, and promotions.

It's hard to define one's work "turf" with defensible physical boundaries in a world of portable office space and telecommuting. Workers have come up with ingenious alternatives for staking out and defending territories that are more conceptual than physical.

The type of manipulation used demonstrates which type of conceptual territory is being defended: information, contacts, or authority.

The first type of territory is **informational**. Is there anyone you know at work whose files are titled and organized so abstrusely that only the original organizer can find his or her way around? Imagine searching for the CommCom company file under "C," only to discover it's sorted under "R" for "red," which is the company contact's hair color. Or maybe you need the specifications for the new project that ten people are working on when you discover that they are encrypted--and only one person has the password.

The holder of informational territory shields access to the information so that anyone else in the company who needs it has to apply directly. Work is slowed or halted if the information holder is unavailable. This person can also control what information is released to the company at large.

The second territory, **associational**, is one of the most easily recognizable of the territories. People at work guard their desktop files as if they were oil fields. Powerful contacts can make and override decisions and provide valuable information. The threat of using a powerful association is usually as effective as actually using it.

Example: associational territory
Henry

Henry makes sure to send at least one "check-in" e-mail a week to the vice president in charge of his department. The two men maintain a friendly correspondence.

Elizabeth

Elizabeth belongs to several professional organizations. She networks extensively within these organizations and regularly calls on the contacts she's made.

Decisional territory is the third, and most competitive, conceptual turf defended at work. Decisional territory defines the boundaries of an individual's authority. Whether the authority the decision maker wields is large or small, it carries significant impact for the workers who are subject to it. Implementing the power inherent in all three territories can be arbitrary, but the power associated with decisional territory is the most frequently abused.

Example: decisional territories in several workplaces

Josh

Josh is the director of development for a software company. He guards his decisional territory by giving the best assignments to the people he favors. Those who work under him are motivated to continuously try to please him in order to get the interesting projects.

Darlene

Darlene, the manager of a customer service center, has a reputation in the office as being obsessively controlling. She insists that she sign off every time there is a deviation from routine. She is frequently in meetings and her absence interferes with the center's ability to function.

Faye

Faye is the director of manufacturing for a toy company. She maintains control over her decisional territory by often changing her mind or overriding other managers' decisions. The people who work for her are forced to be alert and flexible.

From a subjective perspective, it can appear that there's a real advantage to building a conceptual territory in the workplace. But the personal interest of the territory holder often directly counters what is best for the company as a whole and can hinder interfunctional progress.

If it's not good for the company, it's probably not ultimately in the worker's best interests either. Territoriality at work impedes the free flow of information and stifles productivity.

The way people at work function sometimes appears slightly irrational, but if you observe more closely, you may find that it's because they've brought their territorial instincts to work with them in the form of conceptual territory.

Steps for the successful negotiation of workplace territory

Have you ever found your ability to do your job inhibited by someone else's territoriality?

Encountering problems with territoriality is a common occurrence for many people. It takes a lot of energy to keep from intruding upon the territory other people have staked out in the workplace, and sometimes it's just downright impossible.

Since it's pretty much a given that you're going to encounter territoriality, what you need to know is how to negotiate it. In this topic, you'll learn the steps for successfully negotiating workplace territory that someone else is defending.

Here are the three steps involved with successfully negotiating workplace territory that someone else is defending. It's important to follow these steps in order, because they allow you to defuse someone's territorial instincts gradually.

- Identify the territory that's being defended.
- Clarify that you're not threatening the other person's claim to that territory.
- Explain your reasons for being on the other person's territory.

The first step involved in successfully negotiating workplace territory is to identify the territory that's being defended. Basically, you need to understand exactly what territorial line you're crossing. This line is more than the line between departments or divisions in an organization; the line is protecting something that is important to that particular person. So how do you identify what's being defended?

Think of a guard dog that only barks when someone enters his yard but may start to growl when someone's at the fence. You know how close you've gotten to the yard by how much noise the dog is making. People react in pretty much the same way when their territories are threatened.

In identifying the territory that's being defended, you need to observe the actions of the person involved. When does he "growl" the loudest? He may be protecting information or authority that he feels you're getting too close to. You need to identify this territory out loud to him in this first stage of negotiating the workplace territory.

Identifying a territory

The trigger

Art noticed that his assistant, Lisa, got upset when he looked for files himself in the office filing cabinets. She had a habit of hiding the key so he couldn't access the files.

The territory

When Art asked her for the key, Lisa said that she'd find the files. Art knew that the filing cabinets and the information in them made up the territory she was defending.

Once you identify the territory that's being defended, it's important to state it directly to the other person. Art needs to acknowledge to Lisa that he knows that she considers the filing system part of her workplace territory.

When you've identified the territory that's being defended, you need to clarify that you're not threatening the other person's claim to that territory. This second step is an important point in the negotiation process. As long as the other person perceives you as a threat, she won't be open to listening to your explanation of why you're on her territory. In clarifying that you're not a threat, you need to be both friendly and firm.

Be friendly

No one will believe that you're not a threat if you approach the situation aggressively. You can start by acknowledging the other person's authority and by affirming your respect for her position. It's important that you're genuine in this; otherwise, the other person simply feels manipulated.

Be firm

It's not necessary to be apologetic in clarifying that you don't pose a threat. When you're firm, you send the message that you take both sides of the issue seriously and that you're looking for a way to make this work.

The final step in negotiating workplace territory is to explain your reasons for being on the other person's territory. Although these reasons may appear obvious to you, usually the other person is too busy being defensive to be able to realize them. It is often this last step that people overlook, but if you can't provide a reason for being on someone else's turf, then there is no point in trying to negotiate for access to this territory. Unlike guard dogs, people will respond more positively to your presence when they know why you're there.

If you expect the negotiation to be successful, your reasons have to be reasonable. Art couldn't expect Lisa to be willing to negotiate about the filing cabinets if his reason was that he wanted to check her work to make sure she was doing it properly. As with the second step, it's important to continue to be both friendly and firm.

Reasons to negotiate workplace territory
You made the decision

It's possible that you intruded on someone else's territory because someone had to make a decision and the person in charge wasn't there.

You share a need

You might need to be on someone else's turf because there's a project or deadline that you share. Be sure to make that information part of your explanation.

Consider this situation: You're the head of design for a software engineering firm. You need the assistance of Tom, the project director, to do a team productivity evaluation. You need access to the time-reporting logs before you can begin working on your part of the evaluation. You've sent Tom three e-mails asking for this information, and you haven't heard anything in response. You had thought that Tom was willing to work with you on this project, but now you're not so sure.

You've decided to stop by Tom's office to find out what's happening. When you ask him about the time logs, he tells you just to worry about your part of the project and he'll worry about his. You know that you need access to those time logs before you can do your part of the project, but you can also tell that Tom is being very defensive and that it probably won't work if you keep insisting on having the information.

Steps involved in negotiating a particular workplace territory

Acknowledge his territory

Tom has made it clear that he doesn't want to give you access to the time logs, which makes these logs the disputed territory. You say to Tom that you know the information contained in the logs is the responsibility of his department.

Acknowledge his rights

Tom states that the logs are under his control. You then respond by saying that you don't want control of the logs and that you understand why it's important that only one department have direct access to them.

Explain your need

At this point, Tom is a little more friendly. You go on to explain to him that you need some of the information that's in the time logs to be able to complete your part of the project.

Were you able to follow the steps of the negotiation process? You had to start by identifying that the time logs were the disputed territory before you could assure Tom that you weren't looking for control of this information or control of his department.

After all this, you could finally explain to him why you needed the information, which is what had brought you into his territory. Territoriality is a very strong instinct, and it's important to defuse it gradually if you hope to be successful.

Creating Interfunctional Alliances

Are you reaping the benefits of strong interfunctional alliances in your organization?

Even though territorial instincts often compel you to work independently and defend your functional boundary, you can accomplish more and generate better results when you work across functions with other departments or sections.

Do you sometimes feel like you're the only one pulling the load up the mountain? Why do it alone when help is available?

You probably don't want to lose the recognition you'd receive at work for a job well done. But what if you could produce even better results without additional effort? Win-win scenarios might seem cliched, but it's a fact that interfunctional alliances often yield better results for both you and your ally. It's worth investigating the potential results that you and your ally can expect if you work together instead of separately.

Maybe now you're ready to be making use of interfunctional relationships in your organization. Are you going to wait for them to happen and grow on their own? Just remember, sometimes it is your responsibility.

When you make the effort to help someone at work, do you view it as simple altruism? Or do you try to use the situation to your advantage?

Humans possess a natural urge to be generous and help others. That urge is often buried when it seems it will lead to being taken advantage of. But that impression is mostly myth. Being generous with your assistance can strengthen your interfunctional relationships and invite assistance in return from your allies when you need it. In this topic, you'll learn about three helping behaviors that you can use to strengthen your alliances at work: being generous, sharing power, and showing support.

The importance of interfunctional alliances

Are you reaping the benefits of strong interfunctional alliances in your organization?

Even though territorial instincts often compel you to work independently and defend your functional boundary, you can accomplish more and generate better results when you work across functions with other departments or sections.

This results in the alliance being more efficient and more effective at getting the job done than if the members of the alliance had worked separately. Remember that interfunctional alliances seldom happen on their own. Alliances need to be pursued and developed skillfully.

Another important benefit of interfunctional alliances is improved communication throughout the alliance. As the members of the alliance work together, they will increase their abilities to communicate: getting their messages heard and hearing what others have to say.

For every goal that your division of the organization sets, there is at least one other division in the organization that has some investment in this goal. With this in mind, you can begin to understand why interfunctional alliances are so important and beneficial to your organization. In this lesson, you'll explore:

- the results that you can attain through forming interfunctional alliances;
- the strategies for effectively improving interfunctional relationships;
- the helping behaviors that strengthen work alliances.
-

Results obtained through forming interfunctional alliances

Do you sometimes feel like you're the only one pulling the load up the mountain? Why do it alone when help is available?

You probably don't want to lose the recognition you'd receive at work for a job well done. But what if you could produce even better results without additional effort? Win-win scenarios might seem cliched, but it's a fact that interfunctional alliances often yield better results for both you and your ally. It's worth investigating the potential results that you and your ally can expect if you work together instead of separately.

Think about the departments you interact with on a daily basis. Each of those interactions has the potential for greater interfunctional cooperation. In this topic, you'll explore the results you can derive from cooperating across functions with other departments:

- increased information;
- better overall resources;
- more support.

The first result you'll encounter once you've established cooperation across functions in departments is increased information. To fulfill your job, you need accurate and current information about markets, systems, services, or policies. You undoubtedly have your own information sources, but an ally in a different function may have access to different or additional sources that can fill in information gaps or provide confirmation.

By sharing information between cooperating departments, you also save yourself time in looking for information that someone else in another department has already found. In today's fast-paced environment, you don't have an extra hour to duplicate research that's already been done.

Another important result of cooperative interfunctional relationships is better overall resources. When competing with another departmental function, you each lay up your resources separately, whether the resources are personnel, labor, research, stock, or supplies.

Share resources

When you create an alliance, you can share resources, including personnel, and cut down on duplication of equipment and other material supplies.

Share costs

You'll also find that establishing a cooperative relationship will make your budget go farther. You can double up on training and on research costs.

The third result of establishing cooperation across functions in departments is more support. Support is a less tangible benefit of alliances, but there's strength in numbers. When you can depend on your ally to second your recommendations, it increases your credibility and authority and makes the implementation pathway easier. People who are part of cross-functional teams are more likely to form networks with people outside their departments, and this adds to the support the organization experiences as a whole.

Acting cooperatively with other functional areas can benefit you by increasing the available information, making more resources available, and providing you with more support.

So are you still doing it alone? Maybe it's time to start looking into how you can incorporate interfunctional alliances into your organization.

Strategies for improving interfunctional relationships in an interdepartmental scenario

Maybe now you're ready to be making use of interfunctional relationships in your organization. Are you going to wait for them to happen and grow on their own? Just remember, sometimes it is your responsibility.

Interfunctional alliances go both ways. You have to give a little to get a little. There's no magical way to develop interfunctional relationships. As with any relationship, improvement requires some effort. If you're the one initiating an interfunctional relationship, it's up to you to lead the way by:

- taking responsibility;
- showing reliability by following through;
- participating diligently in the working relationship.

In this topic, you'll learn how to apply these strategies for leading the way in improving interfunctional relationships. The skills you take away from this topic will be useful in a variety of inter- and intradepartmental situations.

The first strategy for leading the way in improving an interfunctional work relationship is to take responsibility. Think about your typical response in situations that involve working cross-functionally with another department. When a shared task or problem needs to be handled, do you take responsibility?

Passing responsibility

It's not unusual for someone to try to camouflage the responsibility by making someone else responsible in the early stages of a project, just in case something goes wrong.

Avoiding responsibility

When you're sharing a project across functions, avoiding responsibility is a sure way to make your partner nervous about working with you.

To take responsibility, you must start by being upfront and responsive to the other people on the interfunctional team. If there's something that your department has been responsible for that it hasn't handled, it's your job to claim responsibility for that failure. You can also take responsibility by overseeing tasks that need to be done or by handling problems that have arisen. Overall, taking responsibility means to own your role in the alliance and to forge ahead toward accomplishing its goals.

Although admitting to mistakes or failures might seem to undermine your position in the interfunctional alliance, the opposite is almost always the case. Being honest about your department's strengths and shortcomings builds trust among you and the other members of the alliance.

The second strategy for leading the way in improving an interfunctional alliance is showing reliability by following through. What this strategy comes down to is simple: do you follow through on your commitments? Reliable follow-through is doing what you've promised when you've promised it, and it goes a long way toward establishing trust, an essential component in all alliances.

Demonstrating reliability by following through on commitments

Don't promise what you can't deliver

You undermine your ability to demonstrate reliability if you consistently overpromise. It will be more impressive and do more for building the relationship if you promise what you can handle and actually deliver on that promise, than if you promise more and don't.

Keep track of what you've promised

Forgetting what you've promised is no way to build an interfunctional relationship. Make sure to keep a written record of the tasks and projects you've committed to. Don't forget to include the name of the person or people to whom you've made the commitment.

Tell others when you finish

When you do follow through, it's not a time to be humble and quiet. It's important that the people involved in the interfunctional alliance are aware of what you've accomplished. If they don't get examples of your reliability, they won't have a base on which to build their trust.

Sometimes follow-through involves following up on ideas that arose in a meeting, even if you weren't assigned a specific task. If one of the conclusions of a meeting is that your team needs to understand its client better, then you can follow through by finding out more about the client and its needs.

When you return to the members of your interfunctional alliance with this information, you'll build their trust in your reliability. They know that when you say you're going to do something, you really are going to do it.

The final strategy in proactively building an interfunctional alliance is participating diligently in the working relationship. Participating diligently means that you volunteer to do your fair share rather than letting all the tasks go to someone else or waiting to be asked. Think about what your response might be. Do you volunteer your efforts willingly? Instead of hiding in the background hoping the task will pass to someone else, offer to take on some of the tasks. You might be surprised when your efforts are reciprocated.

Participating diligently in the working relationship also means that you take the goals of this alliance seriously and express your commitment to accomplishing them. No one likes working on a team with others who aren't doing their share of the work.

All the strategies for taking the lead in an interfunctional work alliance are meant to build trust among the members of the alliance. In carrying out the third strategy, you help to move the group from trust-building into action.

Participate in the working relationship of an interfunctional alliance

Decision-maker

Get the jump-start on what needs to be done. If you're a decision maker for the group, pull together the resources necessary to accomplish the group's goals.

Not decision-maker

If you're not a decision maker, volunteer to take the lead on a task force. Focus on the information and decisions necessary for accomplishing the group's goals.

Think again about the interfunctional alliances you've been part of in the past. Could you have benefited from being able to apply each of the three strategies: taking more responsibility, following through, and participating?

Example: Abby is the head of the customer relations department for a financial services organization. She needs to work with the sales department to help expand the company's client base. Mark heads the sales department. He and Abby have never worked together, and Abby is hoping to form a strong bond between the departments that will benefit them both. Abby has prepared a report detailing her department's history and the services it offers to the company's clients. She has brought the report with her to her first meeting with Mark.

What can Abby do to lead the way in establishing and improving the interfunctional relationship between her department and Mark's? Follow the conversation between Abby and Mark as she works to build the relationship.

Mark: I know that any sales job you do will only be undermined if my department fails to maintain the firm's relationships with its clients. My role in expanding our client base will be to create a package that you can present to clients that details the services my department offers.

Abby: I've brought with me a report that details my department's history and the services it offers to our clients. You had mentioned something in a past staff meeting about not having enough information about what my department does, and I thought this might be of use.

Mark: I'm glad to hear that you understand how our departments have to function together. It sounds like you have a solid sense of where your responsibilities lie.

Abby: Why don't we go over this report now, so that I can get a sense from you of what you'd like to see in the final documentation I send to you? We can meet again next week and I'll give you a working draft to make comments on.

Mark: Thanks. I'm impressed that you have such a good understanding of what we need and have already started working on things.

Abby: Sounds good to me. I'm really looking forward to continuing to work with you and your department. I think we'll be able to do a lot for each other.

Did you realize how Abby used each of the strategies to help improve her newly formed interfunctional relationship with Mark? She was very upfront about acknowledging her responsibilities, and she followed through on a past request from Mark for more information about her department.

Abby also demonstrated her ability to participate diligently in the relationship by taking the lead on getting the project underway. As a result of Abby's efforts, Mark looked forward to continued collaboration between their departments.

As you could learn in the situation with Roger, it's possible to turn a strained interfunctional relationship into one built on trust. This isn't always easy when you're working outside the structural boundaries of your department. Learning how to work with more fluid functional definitions and coordinate productively across functions can be challenging. By taking responsibility for your role, following through on your commitments, and participating diligently in the relationship, you'll be well on your way to an alliance that will be successful.

Behaviors that strengthen work alliances

When you make the effort to help someone at work, do you view it as simple altruism? Or do you try to use the situation to your advantage?

Humans possess a natural urge to be generous and help others. That urge is often buried when it seems it will lead to being taken advantage of. But that impression is mostly myth. Being generous with your assistance can strengthen your interfunctional relationships and invite assistance in return from your allies when you need it. In this topic, you'll learn about three helping behaviors that you can use to strengthen your alliances at work: being generous, sharing power, and showing support.

Being generous is the first helping behavior you can use to strengthen your alliances at work. Generosity toward your allies can take many forms, including providing unsolicited assistance with a task or problem, going out of your way to meet an ally's needs, or offering your expertise in an area in which someone else needs training. The ideal is to give without any expectation of return. However, the natural response to a gift is usually to give something in return, so in most cases, you can depend on your generosity being reciprocated.

Joelle had to give a speech at a professional conference. Elaine, one of her colleagues from another department in her firm, volunteered to listen to Joelle practice her speech and to give her feedback on how to improve it. Joelle ended up giving a fantastic speech, and the bond between the two women grew stronger.

The second helping behavior that can strengthen your alliances at work is sharing power. A leader who makes all the decisions often ends up pushing away those people who might have served her very well as allies. In sharing the power of making decisions, you build connections with those allies.

Example: behaviors that strengthen work alliances
Patrick

Patrick runs the design department for a multinational advertising company. He regularly asks the advice of Jane, the manager in charge of the firm's editing crew.

Ruth

Ruth makes a point of asking for input from her department and collaborating departments when she needs to make a decision that will affect everyone.

When you make a show of your authority in a relationship, it can inhibit the potentially useful flow of ideas and initiative. The result is often a response intended only to gain your approval.

If you relate collaboratively, easing up on the authority and sharing the power, it will set a looser, more constructive dynamic that will encourage your ally to participate more freely and helpfully.

The final helping behavior that can strengthen your alliances at work is showing support. When you show support, you need to be present, speak up, and make your support of your ally concrete and visible. You don't have to get behind everything he or she proposes, but supporting your ally in a few select areas to show solidarity can make a big difference for the ally and costs you little.

Example: showing support.
Natalie
Natalie, the head of the transportation division at an engineering firm, spoke up at the executive staff meeting and voiced her approval of Evan's proposal for the new company time-tracking system.

John
John, a vice president of development, wrote a letter to his company's CEO praising the efforts of Anthony and Melinda, both of whom work on the product analysis team and who have interacted with John many times on their current project.

Jeff
Jeff, a senior developer in a training company, told Simon, a new graphic designer, that he would be Simon's advocate on the interdepartmental development team.

Were you able to see in those examples how the third helping behavior operates? Showing your support for an ally is a way of building relationships at both the individual and the team levels.

Strengthening your work alliances can be as simple as following your instinct. Every day, your work environment presents you with a plethora of opportunities. What are you waiting for? Just remember three simple rules.

- Be generous.
- Share power.
- Show support.
-

Strengthening Communication across Boundaries

Communication is not always about what you say, or even how you say it. There's a lot more to communication than mastering media and speaking clearly. That's because good communication is a great deal more than transmitting information.

"Good fences make good neighbors." - Robert Frost, American poet. Not all fences are designed to keep people out. A fence can be a necessary part of collaborating and finding common ground. In the workplace, you often find fences around functional units. Conscientiously building a sense of togetherness fortifies the collaborative efforts that occur across those functions.

Successful communication is largely a function of how well the message fits the ear that hears it. You can't do much to change the ear, but you have a great deal of control over the approach and style of the message itself. The trick is learning how to adapt your message to suit the ear whose attention you need.

Eh? What's that? What'd you say? Speak up, I can't
hear you. When you're working with someone on a
common goal, the most likely way for the project to get
off track or encounter problems is during some aspect of
the communication process. It's easy to make the
assumption that the other person processes information
the same way you do, or understands the words or
conclusion in the same way, but that's not necessarily the
case. In this topic, you'll explore the interfunctional
communications model. It addresses problems in
interfunctional communication and helps get you back on
track.

Improving interfunctional communication skills

Communication is not always about what you say, or
even how you say it. There's a lot more to communication
than mastering media and speaking clearly. That's because
good communication is a great deal more than
transmitting information.

Communication brings people together. Developing a
broad range of communication skills in the context of
interfunctional relationships can help you establish
interfunctional bonds. These bonds add to the alliance's
ability to accomplish its goals effectively and efficiently.

Trust

As you work on building your interfunctional
communication skills, your efforts result in the
development of more trusting interfunctional
relationships.

Cooperation

Interfunctional communication skills also contribute to the group's ability to work cooperatively across functions toward goals.

People will always communicate, but the strength of that communication lies on the strength of the communication tools people have. How strong are the tools you have at your disposal right now? Are you ready to add to what you already have? In this lesson, you'll learn:

- three ways to establish commonality with co-workers;
- the steps involved in the process of adaptive communication;
- the communications skills for improving interfunctional relationships.

Establishing commonality

"Good fences make good neighbors." - Robert Frost, American poet

Not all fences are designed to keep people out. A fence can be a necessary part of collaborating and finding common ground. In the workplace, you often find fences around functional units. Conscientiously building a sense of togetherness fortifies the collaborative efforts that occur across those functions.

In this topic, you'll explore the use of identifying shared goals, defining boundaries, and acknowledging contributions as effective ways of establishing commonality with interfunctional co-workers.

Identifying shared goals is of primary importance when you're working across functions in an organization. In these situations, it's easy for the goals of the alliance to be misunderstood. This makes it worth initiating a conversation or sending a memo to state and verify goals with your allies on the interfunctional team. It's also important to review your goals at regular intervals to assess the group's progress and to verify the continued relevance of those goals.

Isaac is the manager of accounts payable for a large distribution company. He's part of an interfunctional team that includes Tim, a senior sales associate. Isaac and Tim have confirmed that the goal of their team is to establish client payment accountability as part of the initial sales contract.

A second means of establishing common ground with interfunctional co-workers is defining boundaries. These boundaries delineate the differences in functions among you and your co-workers. If you work in programming and your counterpart deals with promotion, finding common ground may seem an insurmountable challenge. Clearly and explicitly defining your individual boundaries - what falls into your common ground and what doesn't-- helps to improve other aspects of the relationship.

Example: establishing commonality
Jim

Jim is a customer service representative for an appliance manufacturer. He's part of an interfunctional team with Cal, a supervisor on the production crew. In defining the boundaries of their positions, both found that the customer remains the central focus.

Loretta

Loretta is the communications director for an international media corporation. She often works closely with Debra, head of sales. After they each clarified the job responsibilities they hold, the two women discovered that they both look closely at consumer trends.

Did you recognize that both for Jim and Cal and for Loretta and Debra, defining the boundaries of their positions helped them to discover common ground?

Acknowledging the contributions of your interfunctional co-workers will go a long way toward firming up the common ground that exists among you. This action carried out in a sincere manner reinforces the cooperative relationship you've established and signifies your continued commitment to the relationship.

It doesn't hurt

Remember that it doesn't hurt your position in any way to be aware of and acknowledge your counterpart's contributions to your combined effort.

What to recognize

You can note solid contributions that significantly help the achievement of your combined goals or recognize an effort that's gone beyond what was expected.

There are many opportunities in interfunctional relationships to acknowledge the contributions that team members have made. When Judith, a software developer, was working with Matt, a graphic artist, she noticed the long hours he put in to get the project to their client on time. After the client responded enthusiastically to the finished product, Judith made sure to acknowledge Matt's efforts in front of the entire staff at the next companywide meeting.

Relationships between neighbors are only as strong as the understanding between them. Identifying shared goals, defining boundaries, and acknowledging contributions enable you to build this common understanding.

Changing communication patterns

"If you want people to change, you must change the way you communicate with them." --T.J. Larkin

Successful communication is largely a function of how well the message fits the ear that hears it. You can't do much to change the ear, but you have a great deal of control over the approach and style of the message itself. The trick is learning how to adapt your message to suit the ear whose attention you need.

Changing the delivery of the message to fit the listener is a style of adaptive communication. In this topic, you'll learn three essential techniques for adaptive communication.

There are three techniques for adaptive communication, all of which you must apply for there to be a strong likelihood of improving the relationship and your success in communicating with a particular person. These techniques are the following.

- Identify incompatibilities.
- Key in on the other person's styles.
- Match the behavior.

The first adaptive communication technique is to identify incompatibilities. To identify incompatibilities, you need to observe and note the circumstances or the situations in which problematic communication behavior occurs. These circumstances may be face-to-face, or they may be through some other mode of communication.

Modes of communication
Written forms

Do you find the communication breakdown in areas such as written reports, memos, or e-mails? It's likely that you have distinct written approaches.

In a group

It could be that your communications with a person are fine one-on-one, but that they break down when you are operating within a larger group.

Grant is a department manager in a food service corporation. He often gives verbal reports at the executive staff meetings. He's noticed that when he's delivering these reports, Andrew, the company chief financial officer (CFO), becomes impatient and stops paying attention.

In the first technique, identifying incompatibilities, it's not necessary to understand why but simply to identify that the incompatibility exists.

The second technique of adaptive communication is to key in on the other person's style. People process communication and information in different ways. It's not difficult to learn how to observe other people's preferred communication styles. Does someone present a lot of detail when he talks? Or does he prefer quick summaries? Do her written reports provide summaries or lengthy tables of contents? What you're working toward is being able to present information in a familiar way that creates comfort and openness.

Remember Grant? His verbal reports tend to be lengthy and detailed. He knows that when Andrew presents a report, it's usually in 30 words or less. Andrew uses the same style when he's giving feedback. On a personal level, he enjoys long conversations, but when it comes to business, it's all about brevity.

In following Grant's story, you've discovered that an incompatibility exists between him and Andrew. This incompatibility is the result of Grant being wordy and Andrew being concise. It's time for Grant to adapt.

Matching the behavior is the final technique for adaptive communication. To match your colleague's behavior, you select a few key components of her style to match more closely. You might change your pace from slow to fast or vice versa. You could try condensing a report into a one-page bullet summary. Matching styles is not the same as mimicking; matching is intended to provide a familiar, easy-to-follow communication that will make your counterpart more comfortable.

Example: matching the behavior

Grant is concise

Before the next meeting, Grant prepares a bulleted report that summarizes what he needs to communicate. At the meeting, he delivers a quick, brief verbal report and offers Andrew a copy of the written report.

Andrew pays attention

This time, Grant finds that Andrew has paid attention to his presentation. In fact, when Grant finishes, Andrew asks him several questions and then compliments him on the work he's done. Grant has been successful in adapting to Andrew's style.

For adaptive communication to be successful, you must employ all three techniques. It is not enough simply to identify what the differences are, or even to understand exactly what the other person's style is. Think of a situation from your own work experience in which you've been unable to communicate with someone. Referring to the three techniques, can you identify one or two ways that you could have adapted your style to meet that other person's?

- Identify the incompatibilities in the communication between you and the other person.
- Key in on the style that the other person is employing.
- Match the behavior of the other person by adapting your style to match his style.

Once you've adapted your behavior to make it more comfortable for others to work with you, they often react by modifying their behavior as well, so the improvement and ease spreads and continues. The only person you can ever really change is yourself, but your changes do have the power of influence.

Adaptive communication is not manipulation; on the contrary, it demonstrates good interpersonal skills. When you adapt for the sake of improving communication, the chances are very good that you will be successful.

You can predict the success of a situation in which someone tries to improve communication by how closely she follows the three techniques. Think back to Grant's story. He was able to improve communications with Andrew because he identified the problem and Andrew's style, and then adapted his style to match Andrew's.

High chance of success

Although there's no guarantee that adapting your style will improve the situation 100 percent of the time, the chances of success are very high.

Refine your style

You may have to refine your attempt to match the other person's style until you are able to match it in a way that works for both of you.

Case Study: Question 1 of 2

Scenario

Angela is the operations director for the Northwestern division of a petroleum company. She's brilliant at seeing the big picture of the organization and keeping her division running on track. Angela believes that an empty desk is the sign of an empty mind, and her office reflects the exciting chaos of her thoughts. She tends to wander when she explains something to any of her colleagues. She's left the last two executive meetings frustrated because Joyce, the chief executive officer (CEO), never seems to give her time to present her report. Angela finds that she's often just getting to the point of her presentation when Joyce is asking her to conclude. Angela is determined that this is not going to happen again. She knows that Joyce is all about efficiency. Joyce has a lot of energy and demands that everyone keeps pace. Before the most recent executive staff meeting, Angela made an outline of her report that highlighted the essential topics. She practiced her presentation for the meeting and found she could cover the highlights in less than four minutes.

Evaluate this situation by answering the questions in order.

Question

As people gathered for the meeting, Angela handed out copies of her report to everyone. Will Angela be successful in finishing her presentation without being interrupted by Joyce?

Options:

1. Most likely yes, because she's figured out how she and Joyce differ in their styles; she's identified the characteristics of Joyce's style; and she's geared her presentation to suit Joyce's style.

2. Most likely no, because her style of thinking and presenting is very different from Joyce's; her thoughts wander when she is presenting information; and she sees too much of the big picture.

3. Most likely yes, because Angela is determined to make it happen; she's put a lot of thought into her own work habits; and she's made an effort to change her method of gathering information.

4. Most likely no, because she's failed to identify the characteristics that are part of Joyce's style, and she hasn't mapped out the possibilities in the combinations of the two styles.

Answer

Actually, Angela has been very thorough about going through all three adaptive communication techniques. It's doubtful that Joyce will interrupt her because Angela's committed to keeping her presentation short and to the point.

Option 1: This is the correct choice because Angela is applying all three techniques for adaptive communication. She knows Joyce is focused on efficiency and covering topics as succinctly as possible. Angela has worked on speaking to Joyce's style.

Option 2: This choice is incorrect. While these are true of Angela, she has also applied techniques to address the communication difficulties. She noted the difference, identified those differences, and tried to adapt to better meet Joyce's needs.

Option 3: Incorrect. While Angela has worked hard, what will improve communication with Joyce is her attention to the three adaptive communication techniques, specifically matching her presentation style to Joyce's communication style.

Option 4: This is an incorrect choice. Angela specifically noted that Joyce keeps a high pace and likes things to be very efficient. Mapping the possibilities of the two in combination is not a technique; matching behaviors is, which Angela has done.

Case Study: Question 2 of 2

Angela is the operations director for the Northwestern division of a petroleum company. She's brilliant at seeing the big picture of the organization and keeping her division running on track. Angela believes that an empty desk is the sign of an empty mind, and her office reflects the exciting chaos of her thoughts. She tends to wander when she explains something to any of her colleagues. She's left the last two executive meetings frustrated because Joyce, the chief executive officer (CEO), never seems to give her time to present her report. Angela finds that she's often just getting to the point of her presentation when Joyce is asking her to conclude. Angela is determined that this is not going to happen again. She knows that Joyce is all about efficiency. Joyce has a lot of energy and demands that everyone keeps pace. Before the most recent executive staff meeting, Angela made an outline of her report that highlighted the essential topics. She practiced her presentation for the meeting and found she could cover the highlights in less than four minutes.

Evaluate this situation by answering the questions in order.

Question

Which are characteristics of Joyce's style?

Options:

1. energetic
2. demanding
3. efficient
4. chaotic
5. absent-minded

Answer

In fact, Joyce is energetic, demanding, and efficient, while Angela is the one who is chaotic and tends to wander in her thoughts.

Option 1: This is a correct choice because Joyce keeps a fast pace and expects others to keep up with her - including Angela.

Option 2: This is a correct choice. Joyce demands that her employees keep up with her fast pace. She demands the same in Angela's presentations by rushing her to her point.

Option 3: This is a correct choice. Joyce likes things to be very efficient and focused. She doesn't like it when Angela wanders away from her point.

Option 4: This is an incorrect choice. Angela, not Joyce, is chaotic. Joyce is very direct and to-the- point, while Angela likes to reflect on her thoughts and often gets off-track in a presentation.

Option 5: This choice is incorrect because Angela, not Joyce, is absent-minded. While Joyce likes to stay right on task and say only what is necessary, Angela enjoys thinking on the big picture and getting lost in her thoughts. She often strays off topic.

Angela paid attention to her observations of Joyce's style and matched her own behavior to that style. By giving Joyce information in a style that suited her, Angela could keep Joyce's attention and succeed in communicating. You don't need to match someone else's communication style every time you interact, nor should you try to match every communication nuance. But when the interaction is important or there's a strong possibility for a misunderstanding, using adaptive communication behavior can ease the situation.

Determining whether the interfunctional communications model was effectively applied

Eh? What's that? What'd you say? Speak up, I can't hear you.

When you're working with someone on a common goal, the most likely way for the project to get off track or encounter problems is during some aspect of the communication process. It's easy to make the assumption that the other person processes information the same way you do, or understands the words or conclusion in the same way, but that's not necessarily the case. In this topic, you'll explore the interfunctional communications model. It addresses problems in interfunctional communication and helps get you back on track.

The interfunctional communications model is built on three components. You can use this model in any communication scenario, but it is particularly important in interfunctional situations. You need all the components of this model to form the base of your interfunctional communication skills.

Be respectful

The foundation of every relationship is built on respect. The more respect you show for others, the more respect they will in turn show to you. In being respectful, you demonstrate your commitment to the relationship and your intention to do what you can to make it work.

Acknowledge differences

There will always be differences between you and others. These differences are what keep relationships vital. It's necessary to acknowledge the differences that exist in a relationship instead of avoiding dealing with them. In acknowledging them, you send the signal that you value such differences.

Listen with an open mind

Communication starts and ends with having an open mind for others' input and ideas. If you're not willing to listen seriously to what your colleagues have to say, then you might as well be working alone. The more generously you listen to others, the more generously they will listen to you.

Remember that every interfunctional team has come together for a specific reason. Whatever the goals a team has, it's essential that the team have a strong grounding in the communication skills that it will need to succeed.

The first component of the interfunctional communications model involves being respectful. A great part of demonstrating your respect for someone is to be direct and generous in sharing your appreciation of that person's contributions. Being respectful is the first component because it is the strongest way to start out an interfunctional relationship and to build on it. If you haven't had any direct experience working with someone, do your homework and find out about her background so you have a basis for showing respect.

Example: Sheila and Terri are both department directors in an energy resource development company. They've known each other professionally for two years, but it was only recently that they began working on a project together.

Sheila knew that it was important to start off this interfunctional relationship with Terri on a positive note.

Sheila: I've been really impressed by your department's record for exceeding client expectations. I know I'm going to learn a lot from you.

Terri: Thanks. I know your record's quite strong too, so I have the feeling we're both going to learn a lot.

Sheila: I'm counting on it. It's a real pleasure to have the opportunity to work with you.

Differences in opinion and ideas are often the result of different contexts and experience. Remember Sheila and Terri? Terri heads up the sales department for the company, and Sheila is in charge of product development. They both have very different experiences. It's also likely that they use different terminology in their jobs.

Example: different experiences

Terri

"I'm in sales, so I think of the product in terms of the end users in the marketplace. I'm used to using nontechnical language that my clients can understand."

Sheila

"I deal with the technical side of the business on a daily basis. I don't know what it takes to sell what I do to clients, but I can explain, in detail, what we're selling."

Acknowledging differences can be as simple as stating those differences out loud and recognizing their existence. It may also entail questioning the other person about his experiences and point of view so that you can determine the differences between you.

Being willing to acknowledge differences leads to the third component of the interfunctional communications model: Listen with an open mind. Any work you put into communication will fail if you're not willing to be open.

You know how frustrating it is to offer an idea, only to have people reject it without ever really considering it. Interfunctional teams are composed of people with a variety of experiences and perspectives, and it's essential that you stay open to hearing what people have to say. While you're not likely to accept every idea you hear, take the time to consider every idea. It's also important to acknowledge the person who contributed the idea. Your goal is to stay open and keep the ideas flowing for the benefit of the relationship.

Example: Karen and Don both lead teams and there's been some competition and a few misunderstandings. Karen is very detail-oriented, but Don prefers to work more creatively.

Don: Hi Karen. I saw your work for the city project and was really impressed. Karen: Thanks Don. You do a great job managing your team.

Don: I have to admit Karen, that while I admire your attention to detail, I'm unable to emulate it. The joint project would probably give both of us the opportunity to express our styles.

Karen: Why don't we begin drafting the overall plan for the project so we can get a good understanding of what we would each be responsible for?

Don: Planning isn't much my style! But I'd be willing to try anything once.

Were you able to follow Karen and Don through all the components of the interfunctional communications model?

- Don started off by complimenting Karen on her work, which demonstrated his respect for her.
- Don went on to acknowledge the different approaches they have to working. He pointed out that both of their styles have a place in this project.
- Don kept an open mind in hearing Karen's suggestion that they begin drafting an overall plan for the project. He also showed his sense of humor, which never hurts in helping someone else feel at ease.

You can examine any interfunctional situation in which someone is trying to improve communication to see if he or she is following the interfunctional communications model. Simply search for all three components in the situation.

As you learned from Reggie's situation, there is a danger in avoiding dealing with differences. You can be too nice and this can harm a relationship just as surely as not being nice at all.

The interfunctional communications model is the basis for building and developing your relationships with those from other departments and divisions. Keep the following three components in mind and you're well on your way to experiencing all the benefits that strong interfunctional relationships can bring.

- Be respectful.
- Acknowledge differences.
- Keep an open mind.

Companies rely heavily on the cooperation of employees from many different departments and divisions. When the relationships among departments are weak, the entire organization suffers. You can't mend old feuds overnight. With what you've learned in this course, however, you can develop your understanding of the instincts and characteristics that underlie relationships between people, and you can develop your ability to communicate and adapt to the needs and styles of those you work with.

Regardless of the product or the service, relationships among people are extremely important in the business world. Remember Alexander Graham Bell's assertion that great discoveries involve the cooperation of many minds.

Interfunctional relationships are your opportunity to experience this joining of the minds. Who knows what great discovery is just waiting to arise in your next interfunctional experience?

CHAPTER TWO

Effective Relationships with Customers

Defining Your Vendor Role

What does your company want to be when it grows up?

Parents teach their children responsibility and commitment, but many companies still haven't learned the value of these qualities. To work effectively with customers, you have to form relationships with them.

You are about to begin a relationship with a new customer. How do you find the information you need?

The most direct route to collecting the information you need is to ask questions: the right questions. The information that customers volunteer reflects their issues and their assessment of what you need to know.

The problem with a "one size fits all" product is that it doesn't fit anyone very well.

Companies usually develop their products or services with an "average" customer in mind. The problem with that is that they will probably never meet that "average" customer. Every customer who comes to you will have slightly different needs or problems. Without reinventing your product line or service, how can you effectively address the individuality of your customers?

"It is not the strongest of the species that survive, nor the most intelligent, but the one most responsive to change." - Charles Darwin, naturalist

Whatever product or service a customer purchases from you, he is always buying results. Whether it's office supplies or a new accounts payable software application, your company knows more about the field than your customer does.

Clearly defining the vendor role

What does your company want to be when it grows up?

Parents teach their children responsibility and commitment, but many companies still haven't learned the value of these qualities. To work effectively with customers, you have to form relationships with them.

Repeat business and customer loyalty are not bestowed by chance; they're earned.

No matter what your business, customers are buying results from you. The results might be a bouquet of flowers if you're a florist or reliable connections and download speed if you're an Internet service provider. Your product or service is simply the way to get the results your customers are seeking.

Before you can effectively develop a relationship with a customer, you need not only to familiarize yourself with your business products or services but also to define and understand what the results are that you're selling.

It's your responsibility to initiate and develop relationships with your customers. But you can't introduce your business properly or develop a viable relationship until you understand your role or roles as a vendor. In the following topics, you'll learn:

•   what questions to ask when initiating a relationship with a new customer,

•   the different kinds of solutions you can offer customers,

•   how to create value for your customers.

Questions that need to be answered

You are about to begin a relationship with a new customer. How do you find the information you need?

The most direct route to collecting the information you need is to ask questions: the right questions. The information that customers volunteer reflects their issues and their assessment of what you need to know.

But customers can overlook information that's vital to your ability to serve them. That's why it's important that you know what questions to ask.

The first question to ask is, "What are the customer's biggest concerns?" If you're selling shoes, you might assume the customer is interested primarily in fit or style. But what if you discover that she's allergic to metal? Or maybe she's adapting shoes into boutique dog toys and wants good, chewy leather with no detachable adornments.

Not all customers fit your assumptions

No matter what your service or product, there will always be potential customers whose needs don't fit your assumptions.

Find out what your customer needs

It sounds simple, but it's a question that is not often asked. Find out what your customer needs and what her concerns are before you begin.

The second question you need to ask is, "What has been the customer's previous experience with these concerns?" After you probe to uncover the customer's concerns, it is important to determine if they are new or ongoing. If ongoing, probe further to find out what the outcomes have been in the past and how they affected the business. This information will help you gain an understanding of the importance of each concern, and its ultimate effect on the customer.

Example: Cynthia, a car parts supplier customer representative, had a conversation with Edgar, an auto detail shop owner. Follow along as Cynthia discusses Edgar's concerns with him.

Cynthia: I'd like to hear what you're looking for in a vendor.

Edgar: Well, obviously, quality is important. Our customers rely on us for good products.

Cynthia: Are there other concerns on your mind about potential vendors?

Edgar: Well, turnaround time is critical for us. It doesn't matter how great the parts are--if we don't have them in stock, we've got a problem.

Cynthia: Would you say turnaround time is your biggest concern?

Edgar: Yes. We've had more bad experiences with turnaround time than anything else.

Cynthia's question about Edgar's previous experience with vendors was key. If she had emphasized the quality of her company's parts but didn't discover that slow turnaround time was Edgar's major concern, the relationship would have ended before it began. You can't persuade customers that you can provide what they need unless you really understand what it is that they need.

The third question is, "What advantages differentiate your company from your competitors?" What you perceive as advantages your company offers may not be important to the customer.

The advantages your company can offer your customer over the competition depend on the answers to the previous two questions, "What are his concerns?" and "What has been his previous experience?"

Example: find out what Cynthia has to say.

Concerns

"The two biggest concerns that Edgar had were quality products and quick turnaround. Our products are high quality, but not dramatically different from our competitors'. However, we've worked to drastically improve turnaround time in the last year."

Previous experience

"Edgar's company had experienced bad situations involving turnaround time. Because it has seen the impact turnaround time can have on customer satisfaction, Edgar's company cares a lot about it."

Each customer will prioritize the advantages your company offers differently because of different needs and concerns.

You need to get to know your customer accurately before you can begin developing a relationship. Obtaining answers to these three basic questions will start things in a good way:

- What are the customer's biggest concerns?

- What has been the customer's previous experience with these concerns?
- What advantages differentiate your company from your competitors?

Types of vendor solutions for customers

The problem with a "one size fits all" product is that it doesn't fit anyone very well.

Companies usually develop their products or services with an "average" customer in mind. The problem with that is that they will probably never meet that "average" customer. Every customer who comes to you will have slightly different needs or problems. Without reinventing your product line or service, how can you effectively address the individuality of your customers?

There are three types of solutions you can offer customers that will customize your products or services. If your company is large enough, it could opt to use all three customer solutions in different situations depending on the customer.

But for any company, adding even one solution to what you offer customers helps to provide a higher, more competitive level of service.

The three solutions approach customer needs in different ways, and it will be up to you to show customers how your solution matches their needs.

When you offer customers a menu of small, independent elements, you subdivide your products or services into smaller discrete units that can be offered in any combination that suits the customer. This first solution appeals to customers watching budgets or with defined parameters.

Examples
Swimwear example
For example, if you sell women's two-piece swimsuits, you might sell the tops and bottoms separately.

Financial services example
If you offer financial consulting services, you can price different elements, such as tax consulting and portfolio assessment, separately.

The second solution of customization is to tailor the core product to customer needs. To offer this solution, there must be a lot of latitude in your product or service, a lot of flexibility built into your procedures, and a versatile and adaptable work group. If you build software, for example, you can build in features for a specific customer. You might use different billing services. Or, if you provide telephone systems, you might build the systems differently for each customer.

It's easier to offer a tailored solution for services than it is for products unless your production process is easy and inexpensive to modify.

Solving the customer's problem is a third way to customize your services. It is a holistic approach that analyzes the customer's need as a problem needing a solution.

Customer want
A customer wanting to post a company Web page might contact an Internet company without knowing exactly what she needs.

Customer solution
The company would analyze the customer's need and put together all the necessary pieces-- graphic design, content, server--to solve her problem.

These three cost-effective vendor solutions address the difficulty of catering to customer individuality. Each model is different and requires a slightly different relationship with both customers and products.

Customize

Many vendors offer customers a menu of smaller, independent solutions that they use to "customize" a perfect fit for each customer. They may use virtual inventories, partners, or record keeping to provide varied solutions and products.

Customizing Example

"My company sells home repair equipment. Every customer has different needs, which can be tough to predict. We partner with other stores that stock similar products. We can use this virtual inventory to fulfill customer needs."

Solve

Many times, customers encounter problems they can't or don't want to solve themselves. Vendors solve the customer's problem. They form a close bond with the customer and provide large, specifically tailored solutions.

Solving example

"I work for a company that produces retail goods. We're really good at production, but we don't have the skills or the desire to do our own advertising. We found a great firm, and we work closely with them as they develop our advertising campaigns."

Tailor

You can tailor the core product to customer need. To do this, you must partner with customers and learn how they work. Then, you'll build your product in a way that fits the customer's needs.

Tailoring example

"We developed a popular spreadsheet program. We worked with a large accounting firm to customize the spreadsheet program to fit into their business model. They don't tailor our product to fit them; we do that for them."

To some extent, the different vendor solutions are simply different ways of describing the same product or service, but having different definitions can make them more accessible to a customer who has a fixed perspective.

Part of working effectively with customers is being versatile enough to meet their needs instead of trying to make them conform to your products or solutions.

Supplemental training services that create value for customers

"It is not the strongest of the species that survive, nor the most intelligent, but the one most responsive to change." - Charles Darwin, naturalist

Whatever product or service a customer purchases from you, he is always buying results. Whether it's office supplies or a new accounts payable software application, your company knows more about the field than your customer does. Instead of selling merely the product or service, you can add value for the customer by offering one or more levels of training along with your product. Three supplemental training services that are easy for you to provide can add a noticeable value difference for the customer using your product or service:

• Educate customers about other potential applications of your product.

• Coach customers in product use.

• Advise customers how to integrate your product into their business practices.

Your product may have a wider range of uses than the ones customers understand. For example, many computers are bought for business purposes, but are also used for entertainment purposes, such as playing music and video files.

Occasionally lists of humorous product uses make the rounds on the Internet, such as one that suggested using a soft drink to clean out a car radiator.

But even the humorous lists can be of service. If you were a soda manufacturer, would you turn away profitable new types of sales?

The second way you can create value is to coach customers about using products. This sounds like common sense, but it's commonly overlooked. Most companies produce user guides or instruction sheets and assume this information is enough. In reality, this is not enough for most people when the product is complex.

You can coach in a variety of ways, including toll-free numbers, e-mail, observing customers using the product, and reviewing how customers have used the product. How can you coach customers on your product?

Finally, you can advise customers how to integrate your product into their business practices. This means showing customers how to make your product part of their day-to-day lives.

Example: Follow along as Sophie, a customer relations representative for a packaging firm, outlines some procedures that can help Theo, her customer, streamline his shipping department.

Sophie: How are the new package materials working?

Theo: Things are going well. They're nice and sturdy, and we haven't had any customer complaints.

Sophie: They definitely get damaged less than other packing materials. Have you thought about changing shipping methods?

Theo: No. Is that something we should look into? How would that help us out?

Sophie: You were using inferior packing materials, so you probably use a very secure shipping system, which often costs more. Now that you have a sturdier packing method, you might be able to save some money on shipping.

Theo: I hadn't thought about that, but it does make sense. I'm going to check into it. It would be great if we could pass those savings along to our customers.

You want to be your customers' expert, not just their supplier. Show them how to improve their business practices.

Any of your competitors can provide the same service or product to the customer. It's the added value you offer that will keep them coming back.

Three consultants had opportunities to increase the customer value through supplemental training services.

Example: learn more about the products they work with and how each consultant used training to increase customer value.

Margaret

Margaret's company sells a call management system that tracks the number of calls coming through the company. For each call, the system permanently records the issue and how the customer service representative handled it.

Leo

Leo's company sells inventory control software. When the product is used properly, the customer should begin to see a better match between product inventory and customer orders. Eventually, the customer will save money by reducing inventory needs.

Kate

Kate's company sells a copy machine that also scans a copy of each document into a document control database. Customers can access information digitally, thus eliminating the need to keep a huge supply of documents immediately available.

Margaret knew her customer well, and she knew customer service representative training was a huge issue for the company. The call management system helped the company track each call and its resolution, important parts of corporate record keeping. Margaret saw an opportunity to help the customer use the same product in a new way.

Margaret showed the call center managers how to pull up the records of each representative. She then showed them how they could use the records to identify training issues for individual representatives.

Leo's customer had different needs than Margaret's customer. The inventory control manager who was using his product needed to learn how to use the product better. Leo devised a system to help her.

Example: learn more about how Leo helped the inventory control manager.

Review

Leo reviewed the inventory control reports on a monthly basis and noted some instances of the product being used incorrectly. He saw a chance to change habits.

Coach

Then, Leo sat down with the inventory manager and coached her on how she could better use the product.

Kate's customer faced a challenge: integrating the product into day-to-day use. Although employees began using the product immediately, they did not change many of their work habits, which meant they weren't getting the maximum benefit out of the document scanning copier.

- Kate spent a half day on site observing how employees went about their work.
- She made a list of recommendations based on her observations.
- She then sat down with the team and identified five ways they could change their daily work habits to get more value out of the copier.

Case Study: Question 1 of 3

Scenario

Steve sells medical imaging technology to hospitals. He has recently sold a brain-mapping machine to a hospital. The machine will be used in different ways by different staff members.

X-ray technicians will use the machine to print out hard copies of X-rays. Nurses will use the machine to record information in patient charts. The doctors will use the machine for diagnosis, and surgeons will use it in the operating room.

Steve's job is to provide supplemental training to the customer to maximize the value of this product. Help

Steve support his customers by answering the questions, in order.

Question

Many of the doctors are concerned about the high cost of the machine, and whether they will be able to get a financial return from it.

What should Steve do?

Options:

1. Steve should show the doctors some other uses for the machine, such as patient education and staff training.

2. Steve should provide a detailed cost breakdown that shows the doctors how the machine will pay for itself.

3. Steve should gather testimonials from other clients about how they've received value from the machine.

Answer

Actually, Steve should educate the client about other potential uses of the product.

Option 1: This is the correct choice. Steve needs to demonstrate the extra value of the machine by covering what other uses it may have. If the machine helps with other problems, the doctors may see the value in making the purchase.

Option 2: This choice is incorrect. The focus of customer training is to help customers understand what results they are buying. By covering benefits the machine has for nurses and X-ray technicians, Steve can demonstrate the value of the purchase.

Option 3: This choice is incorrect. Testimonials won't help the doctors see added value in the machine. Steve can help the doctors understand other uses for the machine that may make the purchase seem more reasonable.

Case Study: Question 2 of 3
Scenario

Steve sells medical imaging technology to hospitals. He has recently sold a brain-mapping machine to a hospital. The machine will be used in different ways by different staff members.

X-ray technicians will use the machine to print out hard copies of X-rays. Nurses will use the machine to record information in patient charts. The doctors will use the machine for diagnosis, and surgeons will use it in the operating room.

Steve's job is to provide supplemental training to the customer to maximize the value of this product. Help Steve support his customers by answering the questions, in order.

Question

The nurses will be using the machine to document information in the patient records. How can Steve best help the nurses?

Options:

1. Steve should train the doctors to do quality reviews on the nurses' work.

2. Steve should observe the nurses using the machine and coach them when they encounter problems.

3. Steve should provide the nurses with training documents that they can review when they have problems.

Answer

Actually, Steve should coach the nurses on how to use the product.

Option 1: This choice is incorrect. The purpose of customer training is to help customers learn how to use your product. Steve is not there to teach the doctors how to do their job. He can best help the nurses through coaching and ongoing support.

Option 2: This is the correct choice. One of the best ways Steve can create added value is to make sure the people directly affected know how to use your product. Coaching and support for the nurses will make the purchase a success.

Option 3: This choice is incorrect. Training documents are often not enough and will not help as problems arise. Ongoing coaching through on-site, phone, or e-mail support will help the nurses use the machine effectively.

Case Study: Question 3 of 3
Scenario

Steve sells medical imaging technology to hospitals. He has recently sold a brain-mapping machine to a hospital. The machine will be used in different ways by different staff members.

X-ray technicians will use the machine to print out hard copies of X-rays. Nurses will use the machine to record information in patient charts. The doctors will use the machine for diagnosis, and surgeons will use it in the operating room.

Steve's job is to provide supplemental training to the customer to maximize the value of this product. Help Steve support his customers by answering the questions, in order.

Question

The X-ray technicians can use the machine to generate printouts, or they can use out-of-date equipment to gather similar, but less comprehensive, information.

How should Steve help?

Options:

1. Steve should show the X-ray technicians how using the machine regularly will save them time and money.

2. Steve should set up a review process to ensure that the technicians are using the machine.

3. Steve should provide the X-ray technicians with documentation on the advantages of the machine.

Answer

Actually, Steve should advise the X-ray technicians on integrating the product into their daily routine.

Option 1: This is the correct choice. By doing this, Steve is helping the technicians see how his machine will improve their practices. This helps the customers realize extra value in their purchase.

Option 2: This is an incorrect choice. Steve can follow up to see whether they are using the machine, but he adds value for the X-ray technicians when he makes an effort to understand how they're using it and how they can use it even better.

Option 3: This is an incorrect choice. Documentation is not enough to help customers use a product effectively. Steve should help the X-ray technicians understand how the machine helps them and the different things they can do with it.

You are more likely to develop an ongoing relationship with customers when you add value to their purchase. When your customers do well, so will you.

Learning Aid - **Initiating the Relationship**

The answers to these questions will help you initiate a positive relationship:

What are the customer's biggest concerns?

Has the customer faced success or failure dealing with the issue before?

What advantage differentiates you from your competitors?

Cultivating Customer Relationships

How does your garden grow?

You don't simply plant seeds and leave them. You have to work on your garden for the plants to flourish. The cultivation stage is essential to any relationship, and there are some cultivation elements that are specific to the relationship between vendor and customer.

If you give a customer what he asks for, he'll be satisfied. If you give him what he needs, he'll be back.

The key to attracting and keeping customers is understanding their needs. No matter how diverse your customers, they all have the same essential needs. Understanding and meeting those needs is the foundation for establishing a long-term relationship with each customer.

Courting a new customer is like going on a date, and with the same goal: You want to meet her again.

When you meet someone you want to meet again, you'll find ways to create a connection. And, if the connection is deep enough, a long-term commitment becomes a possibility. The same principle applies to a new business customer. It's up to you to establish and strengthen the connection by building rapport.

Have you ever set a goal to strengthen yourself physically?

Before you can build strength in your body, it helps to know which muscle-building techniques do the best job. And before you can build strength in your customer communication, you have to know some communication-building techniques.

The value of cultivating customer relationships

How does your garden grow?

You don't simply plant seeds and leave them. You have to work on your garden for the plants to flourish. The cultivation stage is essential to any relationship, and there are some cultivation elements that are specific to the relationship between vendor and customer.

The advantages of developing a relationship with your customers are more than abstract; the value is concrete.

When you cultivate customers, they're more likely to stay with you and do repeat business.

That means each additional customer you cultivate broadens your base. Sales become cumulative instead of independent.

Nothing succeeds like success. The more committed customers you can claim, the better your market position in respect to your competitors. After all, spoken communication from person to person is the best advertising method. Many different types of companies, from automobile manufacturers to clothing retailers, have built their business on committed customers.

Every sale can lead to future sales from repeat customers. Your goal is to keep the customers you have and grow a larger business from the base you've created.

It costs less to maintain customers than to attract new ones. Committed customers: • require significantly less marketing and advertising dollars

- need fewer promotions,
- occupy fewer people hours,
- increase your profit margin.

Cultivating customers takes far more effort than providing a customer service telephone number to keep customers satisfied--but the value shows up in your ledgers.

In this lesson, you'll learn about techniques that can help you understand and cultivate your customers on a one-to-one basis:

- understanding customer needs,
- building rapport,
- strengthening communication.
-

Customer needs

If you give a customer what he asks for, he'll be satisfied. If you give him what he needs, he'll be back.

The key to attracting and keeping customers is understanding their needs. No matter how diverse your customers, they all have the same essential needs. Understanding and meeting those needs is the foundation for establishing a long-term relationship with each customer.

Sorin Dumitrascu

Everyone cares about getting a fair price. It's always tempting to increase the price of products and services, but your customers generally know what the going market rate is--and that's what they've budgeted before contacting you. But you don't have to offer a bargain-basement price to win a sale. Providing a fair price doesn't necessarily mean the lowest price; it means a good match between the value of the product or service and its cost.

You like to be treated fairly, and so do your customers. They'll worry if the price is too low, but inflated prices concern them too.

You may think customers are shopping for your product or service, but what they really need are the results that your product or service offers.

Examples
Computer program provider

"The product I sell is a computer program that tracks inventory, sales, and backorders. My product's results aren't numbers but efficiency. The customer understands her ordering needs and is able to reduce inventory and still meet customer needs. That means the customer's costs are lower."

Printing services provider

"My company provides printing services. We make brochures, letterhead, business cards, and other similar products. We provide our customers with an important result--a polished, professional image. Our costs are reasonable, and we also provide quick turnaround time."

Customer service provider

"My company sells customer service. We provide customer service agents who are trained in specific products and can answer questions 24 hours a day. The result we provide is customer satisfaction. The customer's customers are happy, because they can reach a live service person anytime they need support. Our customers don't have to worry about building a customer service department."

Your customers are shopping for results, but wait until you have all the information before you form an opinion; the results they're looking for may differ from your expectations.

The third customer need is outstanding service. Part of what your customers are seeking is freedom from worry. Your responsive service is their insurance policy.

Example:

Sheila

Sheila can rely on her printing vendor to deal fairly with last-minute changes. She knows her vendor will make changes fast at a reasonable cost.

Mark

Mark knows his network provider will always be there to answer questions, so he doesn't worry about problems he can't solve.

Your customers need service for many different reasons. Sometimes, they need questions answered quickly when they're feeling frustrated. At other times, they need help installing or using your products.

Customers need to know they can go to you to help them solve problems. The support you provide can help differentiate you from your competition--and generate repeat business.

Today, many customers are looking for long-term relationships with vendors. They don't want to constantly repeat the process of looking for and evaluating product and service providers.

Benefits of establishing a long-term relationship for more information

End the routine

Customers don't want to keep repeating a shopping and buying routine over and over. They benefit as much as you do from a long-term relationship. It cuts their costs and saves their energy for more important tasks.

Retain a knowledgeable vendor

A vendor who already knows the customer and his needs is going to be able to supply those needs more efficiently and effectively than a new vendor. Long-term relationships reduce the customer's worries if he can rely on the vendor to anticipate and solve his problems.

When a customer asks for a box of pencils, what he's really asking for is a fair price for the ability to write without worry and the secure knowledge that he has found a dependable long-term source for pencils.

If you offer customers more than a product--if you meet their essential needs--you've sold them your business as well.

Strategies for building rapport with a new customer

Courting a new customer is like going on a date, and with the same goal: You want to meet her again.

When you meet someone you want to meet again, you'll find ways to create a connection. And, if the connection is deep enough, a long-term commitment becomes a possibility. The same principle applies to a new business customer. It's up to you to establish and strengthen the connection by building rapport.

Three strategies can help you build rapport with customers. These are all interactive strategies best applied in face-to-face conversational situations, although they can be applied in telephone conversations and adapted for direct written communication as well:

- Compliment your customers.
- Find commonality.
- Focus on areas of agreement.

The three rapport-building strategies help you establish positive ground with your customer.

Strategies

Compliment customers

Compliments can help your relationships with customers. They want you to notice what they're doing right. Take the time to notice these things, and point them out. Say things like, "You must be doing things right to have such a low turnover rate."

Find common ground

Find common ground with your customer. This lets your customer know you can relate to him. For example, "I went to the state university too. The football team is having a great year."

Focus on agreement

Focus on the things you and the customer agree on, not on areas of disagreement. For example, "I understand your opinion about outsourcing the programming, but it sounds like we really agree about the implementation of the software."

These rapport-building techniques work only with one critical ingredient: sincerity. No matter how much you practice these techniques, if your product is bad, or if you're being deceptive, you won't establish rapport.

Rapport is built on a sincere desire to help the customer. Always remember this.

Recognizing ways to build rapport is helpful. But it's even more effective when you can apply rapport- building strategies yourself.

Compliments are different from flattery. To be believed, compliments must be sincere. To be able to offer a sincere compliment you must accumulate enough information to know what warrants compliments. In addition to complimenting what you already know about the company and what you can observe about the customer, if you listen carefully, you can turn what you learn in conversation into a compliment.

Example

The customer says:

"We opened three new franchises last month."

The vendor turns the disclosure into a compliment.

"Three openings in that space of time is an impressive accomplishment for the size of your operation. You must have implemented some very efficient systems.

The second rapport-building technique is to find commonality. This is the "so do I" strategy, as in, "You use that toothpaste? So do I." You can pursue commonality with a customer on both the interpersonal level and the business-to-business level.

Business commonality

On the business level, you might note that you use the same supplier for some service and share your views on the service he's provided.

Personal commonality

On the personal level, maybe you drive the same make of automobile, or come from the same geographic region, or like the same books.

Court your customers; don't just take their orders. You can start building rapport in a single conversation by:

- complimenting your customers,
- finding commonality,
- focusing on areas of agreement.

Communication techniques that strengthen relationships

Have you ever set a goal to strengthen yourself physically?

Before you can build strength in your body, it helps to know which muscle-building techniques do the best job.

And before you can build strength in your customer communication, you have to know some communication-building techniques.

When you develop a plan to strengthen communication, there are three important building blocks you need to consider.

These blocks are paying attention, soliciting customer feedback, and conveying respect.

These building blocks will help you build a foundation and strengthen your relationship with each of your customers.

Paying attention

Paying attention needs to be an active component of your communication techniques. Paying attention involves active listening so you can communicate your true understanding and ask targeted questions.

Soliciting customer feedback

Seek specific feedback. Ask your customer about product satisfaction, and if it's not 100 percent, find out why--and how the customer would improve it. Be specific and ask about performance within the scope of how the customer has applied the product or service.

Conveying respect

Respect is the basis for the trust and confidence that are required for a long-term relationship. Respect does not imply agreement. That's a separate issue. Respect indicates that you are aware of and value some of the other person's abilities and judgment.

You can apply the three communication techniques independently and in separate conversations, but they're most effective when you find a way to incorporate all three in each interaction with the customer.

You're probably like most people--you want others to pay attention when you're talking. Customers notice whether you're listening. It's critical that you demonstrate your interest in the conversation.

How to demonstrate interest to learn more

Stop talking

"The number one rule with clients is to stop talking. Your customer should be doing more than half the talking, not you. You should be asking about her needs, not telling her what you think her needs should be."

Take notes

"It's a great idea to take notes. The customer knows you're taking him seriously, and you have an accurate record of the conversation. Ask for permission first, but most customers will be impressed by your diligence."

Listen actively

"I use a lot of active listening techniques. I repeat the customer's statements back to him. I make sure I look engaged--I nod my head, lean forward, and ask a lot of questions. This sends the message that I'm paying attention."

What do your customers like about your product or service? What do they dislike? What changes would they like your company to make?

Do you know the answers to these questions? If not, you could be missing important opportunities to improve customer relationships.

You can get the best answers to these questions from your customers themselves.

There are many ways you can gather information about potential improvements from customers. You may choose to implement one method or a blend of techniques.

Methods
Focus groups
You can get groups of customers together and ask for their feedback. Focus groups can be expensive and time-consuming, but they often provide valuable feedback. When you establish a focus group, you'll want to prepare questions ahead of time to guide the group.

Surveys
Surveys are an easy and convenient way for customers to provide feedback. You can include surveys with mailings, hand them out at meetings, or deliver them along with products and services. Although survey return rates are often low, those that you do receive are useful.

Interviews
The easiest way to get customer feedback is to simply ask. Ask customers questions like: "How well did our

product fill your needs?" "What would you like to see change in the future?" "What can we do to convince you that we are the best company to fill your needs?"

Conversations

You don't have to collect customer feedback formally. Sometimes you'll receive the best information in a one-on-one conversation. When you talk with customers, ask for their honest feedback.

An important footnote

It's a great idea to get customer feedback, but it's critical that you follow up with the customers later. Let them know what you've done with their feedback. This is the best way to reward customers for the time and effort they've put into giving it to you.

Example: Follow along as Jane asks Fred, a customer, for feedback about her company.

Jane: We have a few minutes left, and I was wondering if I could check in with you about how we're doing.

Fred: Absolutely. I appreciate that you're taking the time to ask. Overall, I'm pretty happy.

Jane: Great! I'm glad to hear it. Let me ask you this--if you could see anything change about this experience, what would it be?

Fred: Hmm. Well, I guess it would be nice to have a technical services number to call.

Jane: That's an interesting idea. How would that make the experience better for you?

Fred: Occasionally, we have a specific problem that could be resolved quickly, but we can't contact a consultant.

Jane asked for Fred's feedback, and he took the time to give her some valuable insight. It's important that Jane consider his feedback and probe for more information about his ideas.

Later, Jane should also let Fred know how she used his feedback, even if his suggestion isn't implemented. He'll know she took his input seriously.

Cathy overheard a colleague express his concern with a vendor. He complained that the vendor showed "no respect" for him. Consequently, the vendor lost the opportunity to build a profitable and productive relationship.

It's not easy to define techniques for conveying respect. However, it's a critical part of building a trusting, productive relationship with your customers.

Although the art of conveying respect can be subjective, there are some techniques you can rely on.

Techniques

Ask, don't tell

Don't just tell customers what you can do for them; ask them about their needs. When you take the time to understand customers, they'll know you respect them and that there are more than dollar signs when you think of them.

Understand values

What does your customer value? What does she admire about her organization? About herself? Figure out what your customer values, and make sure that's your primary concern in your interactions with her.

Set aside time

The best way to convey respect is to take the time to listen and communicate with customers. Set aside time to listen, and don't allow interruptions to distract you. This will show the customer that you respect his time and business.

Tell the truth

Tell customers the truth, especially when that's hard to do. Customers know how difficult it is to deliver bad news, and they'll appreciate it when you give them the whole truth, especially when it doesn't make you look good.

It is your responsibility to create or take advantage of an opportunity to use the communication techniques with the customer.

Learning Aid - Results Chart

You can use this information to initiate relationships with customers. Here is an example for your reference:

Product – My company provides printing services. We make brochures, letterhead, business cards, and other similar products.

Results – We provide our customers with an important result – a polished, professional image. We also provide quick turnaround time and a reasonable cost.

Learning Aid - Building Rapport

Use the following rapport-building techniques and self-check questions to identify methods to build rapport with your customers:

Compliments – Is the compliment sincere?

Areas of Commonality – Are the areas sincere? Is this area of commonality important to the customer?

Areas of Agreement – Is the area of agreement positive? Do you and the customer truly agree?

Maintaining Long-term Relationships

Does your company appreciate the value of repeat business and customer referrals?

Many companies rely heavily on market surveys and marketing techniques to attract new customers but fail to realize that it's more cost-effective to maintain the customers they already have. Maintaining long- term relationships reduces the cost associated with customer turnover, and it doesn't require large advertising and marketing budgets. It does require a caring professional attitude and authentic personal contact.

"Trust me."

How often do you hear that from someone wanting to pursue a relationship with you? Frequently? That's because trust is the universal factor that supports all commitments. But when you ask for someone's trust, it's not uncommon to hear some skepticism in reply. The only way to earn someone's trust is to show her you're trustworthy. This is as true in business relationships with a customer as it is in personal relationships. So how do you show that you're trustworthy? What is trust made of?

A marriage has a much better chance of succeeding if, before the individuals get married, they assess whether the partnership possesses the elements necessary for a long-term commitment. That's as true of a vendor-customer relationship as it is in a marriage partnership.

You don't have to guess about making a commitment to a customer. You can review the relationship to date to determine if the necessary elements are present.

Your customer service creed doesn't necessarily have to be "The customer is always right," but should be "The customer always comes first."

Being a responsible, customer-oriented company doesn't necessarily mean you should always agree to the customer's demands. It does, however, mean that you should always demonstrate your active support and responsiveness.

Maintaining long-term relationships with customers

Does your company appreciate the value of repeat business and customer referrals?

Many companies rely heavily on market surveys and marketing techniques to attract new customers but fail to realize that it's more cost-effective to maintain the customers they already have. Maintaining long- term relationships reduces the cost associated with customer turnover, and it doesn't require large advertising and marketing budgets. It does require a caring professional attitude and authentic personal contact.

When your entire staff recognizes and supports the goal of committed customer relationships, your company will be better able to anticipate the needs of customers and meet their expectations.

Expanding your market to capacity is always a good strategy, but don't overlook the valuable return from maintaining active, long-term relationships with customers.

Good products and prices may win you customers, but it's your responsibility to maintain the relationship and convert it into customer loyalty. In the following topics, you'll learn how you can retain and advance the relationships you have with your customers by:

- maintaining trust,
- committing to the relationship,
- using long-term maintenance.

A trusting relationship

"Trust me."

How often do you hear that from someone wanting to pursue a relationship with you? Frequently? That's because trust is the universal factor that supports all commitments. But when you ask for someone's trust, it's not uncommon to hear some skepticism in reply. The only way to earn someone's trust is to show her you're trustworthy. This is as true in business relationships with a customer as it is in personal relationships. So how do you show that you're trustworthy? What is trust made of?

The first component of trust is candor. Don't wait to be asked before you volunteer information that could be important to your customers. If you're running behind schedule, don't make excuses--just tell them. Customers may give you a hard time for it, but they'll appreciate being dealt with in a straightforward manner.

Dealing with customers in a straightforward manner

Be forthright, don't cover up

Being forthright with your customers will be more beneficial than trying to cover up and make excuses. Besides, cover-ups tend to have disastrous outcomes.

Candor is simply stating the facts

Using candor doesn't necessarily mean being the bearer of bad news. It simply means stating the facts without embellishment or excuses.

After candor, the second component of trust is consistency. Consistency is the way you demonstrate your reliability. You don't say one thing one minute and another the next. The product that your company delivers doesn't vary in quality, so why should your customer service or customer interactions be any different? Communicate and demonstrate to the customer what to expect at the outset, and that's how you should behave throughout the relationship.

Example: Building trust

Statement 1

"Too often, customers get ignored soon after the selling transaction has taken place. I create trust with my customers by making sure I'm consistent in how I behave and treat them before and after they've purchased our products."

Statement 2

"Being consistent in delivery helps create a trusting relationship with customers. I make sure that our product and customer service meets customer expectations time after time. Trust isn't built when delivery wavers."

Statement 3

"I make sure that I remain consistent in how much attention I give each customer. Our smallest clients get as much detailed attention and service as our biggest clients. This shows we're service-, not profit-driven, which creates a trusting atmosphere."

You don't like hypocrisy, and neither do your customers. Don't say one thing to your customers when you really mean another. And don't ooze false sincerity. Customers will always notice it.

Being authentic in what you say and what you do helps create a trusting relationship. Make sure your interactions with your customers genuinely reflect you and your company.

Trust is the key to every successful relationship. In this topic, you learned the components that can help you build and maintain a trusting relationship with your customers:

- candor,
- consistency,
- authenticity.
-

Long-term business relationship readiness

A marriage has a much better chance of succeeding if, before the individuals get married, they assess whether the partnership possesses the elements necessary for a long-term commitment. That's as true of a vendor-customer relationship as it is in a marriage partnership.

You don't have to guess about making a commitment to a customer. You can review the relationship to date to determine if the necessary elements are present.

Why would you want to commit to a long-term relationship with a customer? Because it translates to customer loyalty. As you devote your energy to meeting a customer's needs more closely, it makes sense that the customer will remain more loyal to you, because you'll be doing a better job of meeting those needs than your competitors. And by now, you know that there are benefits to customer loyalty.

Now that you know why you should commit to long-term customer relationships, the next question is when to commit to such a relationship. This topic is designed to help you answer that question. There are elements that should be present in the customer relationship that can help you determine whether or not you should commit to a long-term customer relationship.

Characteristics of a long-term committed relationship

It should meet the needs of both organizations.

In any relationship, there is some give and take. But for partnerships to truly work, both you and your customer should gain something positive from the relationship. The needs of both organizations should be satisfied by what each brings to the partnership.

Each party should share responsibility for outcomes.

Being committed in a long-term relationship not only means shared resources, but also shared business responsibilities and burdens. If this is already present in your relationship with a customer, you should consider committing for the long-term.

The relationship should be dedicated to the customer's development.

This doesn't mean growth for the customer and none for you. It simply means having an organizational mind-set of wanting to contribute to your customer's growth. It means helping him uncover potential needs that you can help to fulfill.

The most satisfactory commitments result when all three elements are present in the vendor-customer relationship.

lthough the elements of a long-term commitment are clearly defined, deciding whether they are sufficiently present in the relationship is ultimately a situational judgment call.

Your organizational needs are unique. Do the customer's needs match your profile, or do you have to make adjustments that neutralize or negate the advantages?

Don't guess. Some factors to consider are order or service volume, frequency and regularity of orders, and overhead costs. Ask the customer for an estimate of what she will want from you and how often, and assess whether your capacities can meet these needs.

Examples:

Example 1

"I didn't commit to a long-term relationship with one customer because her needs far exceeded my company's ability to produce and meet those needs."

Example 2

"One customer had needs that were so small and infrequent that meeting those orders wasn't profitable for my company, so I didn't commit to him, either."

To some extent, a long-term commitment with a customer is analogous to a partnership. The burden of responsibility should be shared, though not necessarily equally. As the vendor, you take on the greater responsibility. And you want evidence that your customers will not make you the scapegoat for their mistakes or poor management of the relationship.

Example: what you should be asking your customers

Question 1

Do your customers acknowledge when they miscommunicate important information or make last-minute changes?

Question 2

Are problems recurring or occasional?

Question 3

Are the customers willing to work with you to set up a preventative troubleshooting process?

Question 4

Do the customers' actions match their words? For example, if they say they're concerned about improving processes, are they putting in their fair share of effort to improve them?

Dedication to the customer's development is not as unilateral as it sounds. Your company is going to grow and evolve, and you need to know whether the customer's development direction is compatible with yours. For example, if the customer is buying paper from you but plans to move his company's output to an online format in a year, it's a positive change for him--but not a development your paper-

supplying company can support.

Find out whether a customer's proposed development dovetails sufficiently with yours so that you can support and help his development without reservation.

As you're getting ready to delve into long-term relationships with some of your customers, there are some questions that you should be asking yourself to determine whether or not your current relationship with a customer is ready for the next step of a committed partnership. If you can't answer "yes" to all three questions about a particular customer, you should carefully consider entering into a committed, long-term relationship with that customer.

- Are the needs of the customer compatible with your ability to meet those needs?
- Is the customer taking ownership and accountability for some of the responsibilities involved in the order fulfillment process?
- Are the customer's development plans compatible with yours?

Example: Vincent is the director of operations for a sampling company that specializes in providing lists of phone numbers to phone banks and call centers. One of his major customers, a market research organization in the South, has purchased a list of phone numbers from his company for two years. It has consistently asked for numbers in the Southern area and Vincent's company has been able to meet that need. He was recently asked by the customer's vice president of operations to enter into a collaborative partnership.

The customer was prepared to handle all the billing requirements through their offices, as well as take on additional overhead costs for shipping and handling. In turn, they required a more accurate and less expensive sample from Vincent's company. They had plans to expand their research areas to the East and Midwest. Vincent's company already produced a nationwide sample, so the research firm's development plans aligned with his. Based on the input, Vincent entered into a long-term customer relationship with the organization.

All the elements necessary were present for him to do so: current needs of both organizations were being met, there would be shared responsibilities, and customer development was in line with his own company's development.

Case Study: Question 1 of 2
Scenario

Sean is the owner of a men's clothing designing company that produces an exclusive, but limited, line of formal attire. Mary, a buyer for a national department store corporation, has been a customer of Sean's for the last few spring fashion seasons. Her business alone has kept Sean's company busy. Mary's company currently handles all the orders through its own systems, covers overhead costs of shipping and delivery, and pays for delivery damage insurance. Sean wants to expand his department store sales, but he has learned that the department store Mary works for is planning to create its own line of men's formal attire within two years.

Analyze this relationship by answering the questions, in order.

Question

Sean has been considering entering into a long-term customer relationship with Mary's company. Is the relationship ready to evolve into that kind of committed relationship?

Options:

1. Yes, because both Sean's and Mary's needs are currently being met, and future development for both companies is compatible.

2. Yes, because Sean's company is small enough to play a role in the competitive business plans Mary's company has.

3. No, because Mary's company is pursuing a development plan that wouldn't be compatible with Sean's sales growth plans.

4. No, because Sean's and Mary's current needs aren't compatible.

Answer

Actually, the relationship was missing the element of dedication to customer growth. The department store's growth plan wasn't in line with Sean's growth plan.

Option 1: This choice is incorrect. Their development plans are incompatible. Sean wants to expand in precisely the same area in which Mary is considering developing her own line. This may be good for Mary, but it's bad for Sean.

Option 2: This is an incorrect choice. Although Sean can play a role currently, the plans of Mary's company to develop a men's clothing line run contrary to Sean's plans of expanding. Mary's plans will not benefit Sean.

Option 3: This is the correct choice. If the companies' development plans dovetailed, then the two could develop a long-term relationship. However, Mary's plans compete with Sean's plans. Her plans are good for her but bad for Sean.

Option 4: This is an incorrect choice. Their current needs are compatible because Sean provides what Mary needs and vice versa. However, the problem lies in their development plans. Where Mary plans for growth, Sean will lose a lot of business.

Case Study: Question 2 of 2

Scenario

Sean is the owner of a men's clothing designing company that produces an exclusive, but limited, line of formal attire. Mary, a buyer for a national department store corporation, has been a customer of Sean's for the last few spring fashion seasons. Her business alone has kept Sean's company busy. Mary's company currently handles all the orders through its own systems, covers overhead costs of shipping and delivery, and pays for delivery damage insurance. Sean wants to expand his department store sales, but he has learned that the department store Mary works for is planning to create its own line of men's formal attire within two years.

Analyze this relationship by answering the questions, in order.

Question

What questions did you ask yourself to determine whether or not the business relationship between Sean and Mary was ready for a long-term commitment?

Options:

1. Are the needs of the customer compatible with the vendor's ability to meet those needs?

2. Are current overhead costs being split proportionately to the amount the organization contributes? 3. Are the customer's development plans compatible with the vendor's?

4. Is there a trade-off in benefits between the supplier and the vendor?

5. Is the customer taking ownership and accountability for some of the responsibilities involved in the

order fulfillment process?

Answer

Actually, by asking if needs and development plans are compatible, and if customers are being accountable, you can determine the commitment-readiness of a relationship.

Option 1: This is a correct choice. Asking this question makes sure that both parties will gain and that neither will be overburdened by the relationship. In this case, both Sean's and Mary's needs were compatible.

Option 2: This is incorrect. Responsibilities should be shared, although not necessarily equally. Vendors usually take on more of the burden. This question would not help you determine whether both Sean and Mary are seeing positive results.

Option 3: This choice is correct. If development plans are incompatible, then one of the companies will lose out. In this case, Sean's and Mary's plans were incompatible, and he would have lost a lot had he invested in a long-term relationship with Mary.

Option 4: This is an incorrect choice. Although there is some give and take, each company should have positive gains and not feel it is making trade-offs. This question would not illuminate whether Sean and Mary should have a long-term commitment.

Option 5: This is a correct choice. Although the share of responsibilities will not necessarily be equal, you do want to make sure a customer doesn't arrange things so you are blamed for a failure that was her responsibility. This question makes sure the relationship between Sean and Mary is equitable.

Landing a new customer is a heady experience. Rushing into a commitment is tempting when you're still counting up the new orders or adding the additional income to your balance.

However, before you commit, take time to review the relationship to find out if it contains the three elements that are necessary for a successful commitment.

It's not caution, but rather practicality, that rules commitments. You want to insure that your relationships with customers have a strong foundation for success. In this topic, you learned the three elements that should be in place before you commit to a long-term business relationship. If you keep them in mind, your business partnerships will have a stronger chance for surviving the test of time.

Analyze a business scenario from a long-term customer relationship perspective

Your customer service creed doesn't necessarily have to be "The customer is always right," but should be "The customer always comes first."

Being a responsible, customer-oriented company doesn't necessarily mean you should always agree to the customer's demands. It does, however, mean that you should always demonstrate your active support and responsiveness.

Let the customer know on a regular basis that you continue to value her patronage and respect her needs.

There are three elements that must be present in your interactions with your customers to convey your continuing good intentions and help maintain the good will in the relationship you've developed:

- Attend to the customer before the problem.
- Maintain dependable flexibility.

- Advocate on the customer's behalf.

One rule of business you can always depend on states that snags and problems occur no matter how thorough you are. When a customer informs you of a problem, "attend" to the customer before you address her problem. That means that you should listen attentively and respond caringly.

Attentiveness quality
Attentive

Preserving the relationship with the customer is the first priority. The emotional impact of a problem is often disproportionate to its operational effects. When you take time first with the customer, the size and severity of the problem shrinks.

Concerned

Attending to the customer requires that you have a genuine concern about his problem, and a sincere desire to be of help. A sympathetic voice can be the difference between keeping the customer as happy as possible or making them more angry while you are finding a solution.

Helpful

You may feel that being sympathetic with a customer and facilitating further solutions is not the concern of your business, but you're wrong. The customer is the first concern of every business. His problems are also your problems.

Thorough

One common mistake that you should take care not to make is to start implementing solutions to the problem without having a thorough understanding of its nature and scope. You may end up creating more problems instead of solving the original one.

Along with attending to the customer before dealing with the problem, another key element to maintaining long-term customer relationships is to maintain dependable flexibility. Repetitious cycles that start out responsively freeze into rigid procedures all too easily.

Methods for maintaining flexibility

Creativity and flexibility

"In my attempt to find a solution to my customer's problems, I make sure I'm as creative and flexible as I was during the original transaction."

No limits

"This means that I'm putting no limit to the extent our company will go to find a solution. If it means starting from the beginning, I'll do it."

Example: Follow along to learn how Lucinda, the manager of a floral shop, maintains a relationship with Irene, one of her customers.

Lucinda: I'm sorry the arrangements aren't what you had expected. They are, however, what you ordered through our Web site's ordering service.

Irene: Please don't get me wrong--they're beautiful. But the colors are wrong. These arrangements are for a wedding reception, and the bride was very specific about her colors.

Lucinda: That's completely understandable. I was very particular about the colors at my wedding too. But we had color pictures of the arrangements on the Web site. I'm not sure how we went wrong.

Irene: Do you see that you used more pink roses than melon-colored ones? I know I'm being picky, but it looked the other way around in the pictures.

Lucinda: As you said, it's a very minor detail. Perhaps it can be overlooked. I can offer you a price discount if you'll take the arrangements as they are.

Irene: I'd love to if it were up to me, but the bride is very particular about how everything looks.

Lucinda: OK. What if we took out a few of the pink roses and replaced them with some melon-colored snapdragons or irises? The less-costly flowers will offset the price of the labor of redoing the arrangements.

Irene: That seems like a reasonable solution to me.

Did you notice how Lucinda remained flexible? First, she was willing to lower her price for the arrangements. Then she was flexible about redoing the arrangements. Develop this type of flexibility with your customers.

One last thing to note about remaining flexible: Your customers' needs change over time. Watch out; don't get lulled into a routine that you easily can't change to accommodate new circumstances. It's important to the relationship that customers can depend on you, but you should build in some flexibility as well. A procedure that was originally developed to support a customer can chase away that same customer if her needs change. So be ready to change with her.

The last element that should be present to maintain long-term customer relationships is to advocate on the customers' behalf. Always speak well of your customers and support them publicly. If you have any differences, address and resolve those privately. You betray your customers' good faith by default when you don't advocate on their behalf. Advocacy can mean deflecting credit toward your customers, defending a position, or praising them for accomplishments.

Create customer advocacy alignment within your organization as well as without. Attitude shows, and your organization's attitude should reflect its commitment to customer support.

Case Study: Question 1 of 2

Scenario

Kenneth was the contact person for a company who bought a video conferencing system from his company. The customer contacted Kenneth to inform him that some of the video cameras were ineffective and demanded that a replacement system be installed. Before trying to implement a solution, Kenneth calmly and attentively listened to the client's problem: Not all the people within the conference room could be viewed at once by a satellite location. Kenneth explained to his customer that the system itself wasn't the problem and that he had several easy solutions to the problem. He could offer a rebate if the zooming capabilities weren't crucial, or he could order special lenses for the cameras, or the current cameras could be remounted for a better wide shot. After the customer ultimately decided to order the lenses, Kenneth reiterated his support of that choice and again voiced his encouragement of the customer's goal of using the latest technology in his business.

Define Kenneth's relationship to the customer by answering the questions, in order.

Question

Did Kenneth effectively interact with the customer to maintain a long-term customer relationship with him?

Options:

1. Yes, because he listened carefully before offering solutions, had several options for the customer, and then supported the customer's choice.

2. Yes, because he efficiently solved the customer's problems without demonstrating unnecessary personal touches.

3. No, because he let the customer decide the solution. He should have been more pro-active in taking interest in the customer by offering one singular definitive solution.

4. No, because he didn't offer to replace the system as the customer originally requested.

Answer

Kenneth effectively used all three relationship-enhancing elements to help maintain a long-term relationship with his customer.

Option 1: This is the correct choice. Kenneth's actions demonstrated a customer-oriented approach. He conveyed his continuing good intentions and helped maintain goodwill in the relationship.

Option 2: This is an incorrect choice. Although Kenneth did solve the customer's problems efficiently, it was his personal care that will help maintain the relationship. Kenneth listened carefully, offered several options, and supported the customer's choice.

Option 3: This is an incorrect choice. By offering multiple solutions, Kenneth remained flexible to the customer's needs and didn't impose a solution on her. This demonstrated care for the customer and allowed a customized solution.

Option 4: This is an incorrect choice. Being customer-oriented and responsible doesn't necessarily mean Kenneth should agree to the customer's demands. He was attentive and supportive, which helped both parties better understand their needs.

Case Study: Question 2 of 2

Scenario

Kenneth was the contact person for a company who bought a video conferencing system from his company. The customer contacted Kenneth to inform him that some of the video cameras were ineffective and demanded that a replacement system be installed. Before trying to implement a solution, Kenneth calmly and attentively listened to the client's problem: Not all the people within the conference room could be viewed at once by a satellite location. Kenneth explained to his customer that the system itself wasn't the problem and that he had several easy solutions to the problem. He could offer a rebate if the zooming capabilities weren't crucial, or he could order special lenses for the cameras, or the current cameras could be remounted for a better wide shot. After the customer ultimately decided to order the lenses, Kenneth reiterated his support of that choice and again voiced his encouragement of the customer's goal of using the latest technology in his business.

Define Kenneth's relationship to the customer by answering the questions, in order.

Question

Match each relationship maintenance element with one or more examples of how Kenneth demonstrated each element.

Options:

A. Attend to the customer before the problem.

B. Maintain dependable flexibility.

C. Advocate on the customer's behalf.

Targets:

1. He offered solutions only after listening to the problem.

2. He offered three solutions to the customer.

3. He supported the client's decision.

4. He reiterated his support of the client's business goals.

5. He listened attentively to the problem.

Answer

Being able to identify these elements will help you use them in interactions with your customers.

By listening to a description of the real problem, Kenneth was attending to the customer's real needs. This allowed him to develop solutions that solved the actual, not perceived, problem.

When Kenneth offered more than one solution, it gave the customer flexibility to determine which one fit her needs best. Without that flexibility, the customer would be left with limited options, which would leave unmet needs.

By supporting the client's decision, Kenneth is actually advocating for the customer. He is giving her public support and praising her for her accomplishment. This is an act of good faith that builds relationships.

Reiterating support for the customer's goals is a way of advocating for her. When Kenneth stated his support, he demonstrated good faith and demonstrated his commitment.

By listening attentively, Kenneth is responding to the customer before the problem. He is paying attention to her before he offers solutions. This helps him calmly address the problem and offer effective solutions.

Once you've invested the effort to develop a firm working relationship with a customer, relationship maintenance requires less effort. But it's important to continue the maintenance; you risk losing the relationship, or even the customer, for lack of attention. The three maintenance elements are simple enough to implement:

- Attend to the customer before the problem.
- Maintain dependable flexibility.
- Advocate on the customer's behalf.

Developing and maintaining effective relationships with customers should remain a constant focal point for any enterprise. It's a rare business that doesn't depend in some manner on its customers for its existence. Working effectively with your customers not only makes good business sense, it could also ensure your business survival.

CHAPTER THREE

Effective Intercultural Relationships

Embracing Cultural Differences

It's tempting to place people and cultures in categories. It makes life easier, right? But it is a generalization to assume that everyone in the world can fit into a neat, easy-to-understand classification. The shallow assessment of a group of people and its culture results in miscommunication and misunderstanding. As Whitehead observed, life is all details. And you would be denying yourself and others a substantive relationship if you didn't look deeper to recognize and embrace those details, or differences, that make people unique.

"I wonder if I shall fall right through the earth! How funny it'll seem to come out among people that walk with their heads downwards!" - Alice, in "Alice In Wonderland"

In Lewis Carroll's book "Alice in Wonderland", Alice had an eye-opening experience and learned there are different realities at play in the world. Her myopic view of life was forever changed and enriched by recognizing these variations.

Discrimination is a perception of an event or a person. This perception often prompts a person to form a judgment. And that judgment can result in a form of prejudice. It is unfair to the party or parties discriminated against, and it is unfair to the organization that needs to find the best people for the job in order to survive. In fact, studies show that the actual differences among cultural groups seldom relate to the perceived differences on which discrimination is often based. As such, discrimination has no place in your organization.

An interviewer once asked American poet Carl Sandburg to reveal his least favorite word in the English language. His response was quick: "Exclusive."

If you've ever moved to a new city or started a job where you didn't know anyone, you might find it easy to relate to Sandburg's answer. He understood how a culture that excludes others negates and undermines its integrity and worth. A community flourishes only when it includes the views and talents of every member; otherwise, it becomes simply a collection of individuals working toward separate and, ultimately, lesser goals. This principle applies to the community in which you work.

The importance of embracing cultural differences

"We think in generalities, but we live in details." -- Alfred North Whitehead, British philosopher

It's tempting to place people and cultures in categories. It makes life easier, right? But it is a generalization to assume that everyone in the world can fit into a neat, easy-to-understand classification. The shallow assessment of a group of people and its culture results in miscommunication and misunderstanding. As Whitehead observed, life is all details. And you would be denying yourself and others a substantive relationship if you didn't look deeper to recognize and embrace those details, or differences, that make people unique.

How does this relate to the workplace? Embracing the differences that exist among cultures is important because the global marketplace is multicultural. From huge multinational corporations to small businesses, all must compete for market share all over the world. With that mix of people and cultures working together, a second reason to embrace cultural differences surfaces: Most businesses are now culturally integrated. Do you know of any corporation that doesn't have a significant cultural mix?

With this integration of cultures, the third reason to embrace different cultures presents itself: It improves understanding of different perspectives. The result of this embrace is a cohesive environment that relies on, and takes advantage of, the potential these varying viewpoints offer.

Before you can build effective intercultural relationships, you need to understand the differences that exist and find ways to bridge them. In this lesson, you will learn how to:

- notice cultural differences,
- recognize types of discrimination,
- facilitate inclusivity.
-

Ways in which cultural behaviors can vary

"I wonder if I shall fall right through the earth! How funny it'll seem to come out among people that walk with their heads downwards!" - Alice, in "Alice In Wonderland"

In Lewis Carroll's book "Alice in Wonderland", Alice had an eye-opening experience and learned there are different realities at play in the world. Her myopic view of life was forever changed and enriched by recognizing these variations.

Now relate her experience to your life. Do you work or associate with people who hail from "realities" different from the one you are familiar with? Do you even notice the differences?

Sure, humans have many traits in common, and it's easy to assume these surface similarities are enough to establish meaningful intercultural relationships. But they aren't. To truly connect with others, open your eyes to the differing realities that make up this diverse world.

Building effective and meaningful intercultural relationships begins with recognizing the differences. In this topic, you will examine areas in which cultures often vary. You will notice cultural differences in:

• appearance
• information organization • social perspectives
• core values.

The first cultural variable is appearance. The way we dress is a significant indicator of the culture we live in. What do you see when interacting with others? Upon first glance, you will see a person's preferred style of dress, the colors worn, the hairstyle, even the marking on her skin. For many, the choices made in regard to appearance often reflect more than fashion; they can also express cultural or religious heritage.

Consider an article of clothing such as the turban. To many, the turban is more than an item worn to protect a man from the sun. Depending on the shape, color, and size, it can tell you where the person who is wearing it lives, what he does for a living, and what his social status is.

The way information is organized is a second cultural variable. The preferences we exhibit when we deliver, view, and absorb information are directly related to our culture. How do you prefer your information to be organized? If you're given a report or an article, do you prefer the information to be presented in a swift, no-nonsense manner? Do you focus mainly on the words written on the page? Or do you take into account the peripheral elements as well?

Content

Content cultures prefer visual, verbal, and written communication. They like detailed information that is communicated in a direct manner. Content cultures include English, Scandinavian, and Germanic-speaking societies.

Context

The majority of other societies, including Latin, Asian, and Arabian cultures, can be classified as context cultures. They focus on the information that surrounds the details, including the ambience and the individual delivering the information.

Meaningful intercultural relationships rely on the exchange of accurate information. To keep information from being misunderstood, consider your colleague's preference for absorbing information.

It also helps to recognize the third cultural variable: social behaviors.

Every culture has its own code of behavior that governs its interactions and relationships. If you've ever visited another country or spent any time living in a culture different from your own, it is these social norms that you notice first. Whereas some cultures consider a quiet, courteous demeanor during a social interaction a sign of respect, other cultures find it insulting if you don't raise your voice and emote.

Example - Brianna and Harold are marketing consultants. They have traveled the world and recently shared their experiences as they prepared for a trip together.

Brianna: I am constantly amazed at the differences in behavior I witness in my travels. There are differences in every action. Even the way we greet others is different depending on the culture you're interacting with.

Harold: That is so true. When I greet someone in Italy, I know I'm going to get a lot of physical contact, and I'm careful not to use the person's first name until he uses mine.

Brianna: You know in Botswana, there are two ways to greet someone. With a person you haven't met before or with a superior, you shake with your right hand; with friends, you shake with your right hand with your left hand clasped around your right wrist.

Harold: There's also the issue of acceptable topics of conversation. I was in England last year, and whenever I brought up the subject of politics I was met with silence. Politics just isn't a preferred topic of conversation there.

Brianna: I was in Moscow last month, and they wanted to talk about nothing but politics. Public behavior is a real sensitive area when it comes to codes of conduct. In Japan and Norway, for instance, I never show any public display of affection or physical contact.

Harold: If you've ever been to Korea, you know how important it is to show respect for the elderly. I make sure to stand and bow slightly when a senior citizen enters the room.

Brianna: You have to pay attention, watch and listen, all the time.

Brianna and Harold have learned to keep an attentive watch on the intricacies of cultural behavior. Whether greeting, conversing, or encountering others in public, all cultures have their own particular ideas of appropriate conduct.

Nearly every facet of a culture's actions, preferences, and behavior can be sourced to the fourth cultural variable: its core values. A culture's core values are the collective philosophy it promotes and preserves in its everyday life. Of course, pinpointing what a whole society values can be a lot like nailing water to a wall-- difficult. All cultures share a similar value for spiritual fulfillment, family preservation, and economic security. Within these commonalities, traits and characteristics emerge that reveal a culture's core values.

Latin Americans, for example, tend to place a strong emphasis on the family. Everyday activities might be prioritized to place familial needs first and foremost.

Much like observing seemingly identical snowflakes fall during a winter storm, the person watching attentively comes to discover their differences upon closer examination. And once you notice the differences, you will never look at the snow the same way again. Don't let the broad similarities keep you from identifying the significant differences that mark a culture's way of life.

In this topic, you learned to recognize four variables that distinguish a culture: appearance, information organization, social behaviors, and core values.

Types of discrimination that occur in the workplace

You've heard about it. You know it exists. You might even know people who practice it. But honestly, do you know exactly what discrimination is?

Discrimination is a perception of an event or a person. This perception often prompts a person to form a judgment. And that judgment can result in a form of prejudice. It is unfair to the party or parties discriminated against, and it is unfair to the organization that needs to find the best people for the job in order to survive. In fact, studies show that the actual differences among cultural groups seldom relate to the perceived differences on which discrimination is often based. As such, discrimination has no place in your organization.

The labor market definition of discrimination is: the valuation in the labor market of personal characteristics of the worker that are unrelated to productivity.

To move beyond the limits of discrimination, you need to recognize the forms it takes. In this topic, you will learn about three types of discrimination practiced in the workplace:

- personal prejudice,
- statistical discrimination,
- biased self-interest.

The first type of discrimination is personal prejudice. This form of discrimination takes place when a person makes decisions based on a preference for one group over another. When it comes to hiring for specific positions, this attitude can be found in employers, employees, and customers alike.

Gina is a technical support manager for a large telecommunications firm. She has seen personal prejudice in action. She has discovered firsthand how it can come from both employees and customers.

Example - learn more about what Gina has experienced.

Employees

"I dealt with an executive who preferred to hire only men for certain field support positions, even though I found women who were more qualified."

Customers

"Customers can exhibit this discrimination too. Many complain when a woman shows up to repair their phone lines. Again, they think men are more qualified."

The result of personal prejudice is that it bars a group of people from making a living based on a person's unfair preference of one group over another.

The second type of discrimination found in the workplace is statistical discrimination. This model of bias surfaces when an employer uses assumed group characteristics to rate individual applicants. This might be a belief that any given female employee will take more sick leave than her male counterpart, or a graduate of a prestigious school is better educated than one from a less prestigious school, or a member of one ethnic group is more ambitious than a member of another.

This often happens in jobs that offer an evaluative test to screen candidates. The employer might not trust the validity of the test and compensate by making a judgment based on statistical information. Despite the test score, he hires the person who fits his subjective criteria.

The third type of discrimination is biased self-interest. This predisposition concerns people who make choices on hiring or promoting based solely on perceived self-interest, such as a preference to work with a particular group over another, despite the employee's or organization's best interests.

This can result in a lopsided preference for or bias toward a particular group.

Enrique is a graphic designer for a literary magazine. He experienced biased self-interest at his last job. He eventually left because he was never able to advance in the company, which was a result of having a supervisor who promoted others from his own group.

Example - select each prejudice type to learn more from Enrique.

Company-wide prejudice

"The whole company nurtured the sort of prejudice in which supervisors favored their own groups over others."

Individual prejudice

"My supervisor knew this and used it to his advantage by promoting people who hailed from his own culture, regardless of skill and talent."

It's natural to generalize. Placing people into broadly drawn categories makes understanding a complex world a lot easier. Unfortunately, this oversimplification fails to provide a realistic picture. In the end, the people discriminated against, as well as your company, suffer.

In this topic, you learned three types of discrimination evident in the workplace: personal prejudice, statistical discrimination, and biased self-interest.

Inclusivity techniques in an intercultural business relationship scenario

An interviewer once asked American poet Carl Sandburg to reveal his least favorite word in the English language. His response was quick: "Exclusive."

If you've ever moved to a new city or started a job where you didn't know anyone, you might find it easy to relate to Sandburg's answer. He understood how a culture that excludes others negates and undermines its integrity and worth. A community flourishes only when it includes the views and talents of every member; otherwise, it becomes simply a collection of individuals working toward separate and, ultimately, lesser goals. This principle applies to the community in which you work.

Anyone can feel excluded when he finds himself in an organization where his cultural background is in the minority. It can often take months, even years, for an employee from a minority culture to feel comfortable with his associates. Thus his talents, skills, and unique perspectives are underused. An organization can alleviate the stress and pressure of a new hire's orientation by using some easy techniques to help him feel like he's an important part of the organization.

Your organization needs to include everyone to achieve its full potential. In this topic, you will learn how to include employees from minority cultures through mentoring, encouraging the identification process, and valuing individual experiences.

The wise organization clears a path for those who need assistance integrating with its community. Partnering the employee with a seasoned veteran, acknowledging his unique perspectives, and communicating how his values tie in to the organization's vision can accomplish this.

Mentoring

A mentor's role is to show the new hire or transfer how to do the job and acclimate him to the organization's culture, politics, and processes. This helps reduce the new person's feelings of powerlessness and ease his access to other members of the organization.

Promoting the identification process

The identification process allows new hires or transfers to become connected to the value system of the organization. Identification also helps the new person develop a meaningful relationship with the organization as well as anchor members within the system.

Valuing individual experiences

It is important to realize that the new hire or transfer from a different culture has individual experiences that are applicable to and can be just as effective as the ones supported and practiced in the organization.

Inclusivity begins with an open door. Mentoring, identifying common values, and listening to different perspectives will help an employee from a different culture become acclimated and feel connected to your organization's community.

But now that the door is open, what happens next? How do you use these techniques?

An effective inclusivity strategy involves support, communication, and encouragement. When properly applied, the result is a new employee who finds it easier to connect, participate, and ultimately produce in a positive fashion.

An effective approach to making this technique work.

Assigning an appropriate mentor

It is important to assign a mentor of the same culture and gender as the new hire. A mentor who shares these commonalities will be more intimate with the organizational barriers the new person faces and be able to provide more meaningful guidance.

Encouraging the identification process

Organizational identification is a personal process. But it can be greatly encouraged by expressing that the organization shares common values and goals with its members. It also helps to use "we" language when talking to the new hire about the organization.

Valuing individual experiences

When someone from a different culture joins an organization, his perspective, learning style, and approach may deviate from the organizational norm. When you see him performing a task in a new way or hear him share information, be sure to offer encouragement.

Example - Eden is from the Philippines. She was recently hired as a financial manager. Her supervisor, Mel, met with her to discuss Eden's early performance.

Mel: Eden, I've paired you with Brian. He's in finance, like you, and has been with us for years so he knows the job well. I think he'd be a great mentor for you.

Eden: Thanks. I'm looking forward to meeting him.

Mel: Brian was also born and raised around here, so he'll be able to point you in the right direction if you need help. I also want to remind you about our training curriculum for the next quarter. I think you'll find some interesting classes being offered.

Eden: That sounds great. Constant learning is really important to me. It's nice to see you have this sort of program available.

Mel: I'm glad you think so. We place a strong emphasis on improving our skills here.

Eden: I can tell.

Mel: Which reminds me: I was looking over your report and I noticed the cash management strategy you suggested. I thought it was very interesting. We've never tried an approach like that before, and I'd love for you to share your insights on it.

Eden: Sure. It's a style I've used often in the past. I hope it'll fit with your current scheme.

Mel is well on his way toward ensuring that Eden feels comfortable with the organizational culture. But based on the conversation that took place, did he use all three techniques effectively?

Mel effectively encouraged Eden's identification with the organization by identifying and expressing a shared value surrounding constant training. Mel also used "we" language that helped Eden feel like she was part of the group. And Mel supported and encouraged Eden's different approach to cash management. By asking Eden to share her insights at the next meeting, Eden received the message that her unique ideas were welcome.

However, Mel could have chosen a more appropriate mentor for Eden. It is important to assign someone from the same culture and gender. If there isn't someone available from a similar background, at least make certain the mentor is from the same gender.

An organization needs to operate as effectively as possible. Your inclusivity efforts will help ease the transition for newcomers and make the experience a positive and productive one for all those involved.

In this topic, you learned how to make new hires from differing cultures feel included by assigning an appropriate mentor, encouraging the identification process, and valuing individual experiences.

Meaning in Context

You arrive wearing formal clothing and hand over a ticket at the door. As you enter, there's a stage up front with a curtain pulled, an auditorium full of seats facing the stage, and musicians tuning up in an orchestra pit.

The lights go down, the curtain goes up, and two teams of uniformed football players come on stage and begin a football game. "Wait a minute," you say. "This is a theater, and I was expecting a musical performance."

"People see the world not as it is, but as they are." --Al Lee, 19th century brigadier general

The world's cultures vary greatly and have a profound effect on people's perceptions. Your nationality, cultural roots, and local customs impact your view of reality. These differences in perception influence the way you orient yourself to the world. For example, time is a reality all cultures readily acknowledge, but how they approach it can differ greatly.

There's a message with every movement. Do you know the message you're sending?

Psychological research of business communication has determined that while 80 percent to 90 percent of meeting time is devoted to verbal discussion, only 20 percent or less of the actual message is conveyed through the spoken word. That means up to 80 percent of the meaning is communicated by nonverbal elements. Just as spoken language varies by culture, so do the nonverbal elements of communication.

Whether it is an advertisement, a report, a stop sign, a tone of voice, or even the way a room is decorated, everything has a message. Almost every expressed thought or action tells you something about the sender, and the receiver. The question is: Do you get the message?

"Go ahead; make my day." - Clint Eastwood as policeman "Dirty" Harry Callahan in the 1983 film "Sudden Impact"

Eastwood's now-classic line is a perfect example of contextual communication. That is, the meaning of the words is almost entirely dependent on the situation that surrounds it, who is delivering the message, and the manner of the delivery--in this case, his character was holding a pointed gun and has a reputation as a policeman who shoots a lot of bad guys.

Cultural communication styles

You arrive wearing formal clothing and hand over a ticket at the door. As you enter, there's a stage up front with a curtain pulled, an auditorium full of seats facing the stage, and musicians tuning up in an orchestra pit.

The lights go down, the curtain goes up, and two teams of uniformed football players come on stage and begin a football game. "Wait a minute," you say. "This is a theater, and I was expecting a musical performance."

You were shocked to see a football game conducted on a theater stage. Why? Because you attribute meaning to setting and context. You expect to attend a football game in casual attire, in an outdoor arena with seats surrounding a playing field.

If you entered a room in an unfamiliar building in an unknown country and saw everyone else there taking off his shoes, what would you expect? A bath? A foot massage? A formal dinner?

Every culture attributes meaning to setting and context. It's a shared form of communication that helps people know what type of situation they're in and what's expected. But if you're not familiar with the contextual meanings of a culture, it can be like trying to paint when you're colorblind.

But the forms, symbols, and content of communication have to be mutually understood. How ideas are exchanged interculturally involves far more than just literal spoken words.

Each culture has nonverbal dimensions of shared perceptions and behavior that carry as much meaning as words do.

There are many ways to say the same thing. The challenge is finding the key to a culture's approach. In this lesson, you will learn varying approaches cultures take when communicating:

- understanding perceptual variations,
- understanding nonverbal expression,
- communicating in content cultures,
- communicating in context cultures.
-

Perceptual variations in cultural norms

"People see the world not as it is, but as they are." --Al Lee, 19th century brigadier general

The world's cultures vary greatly and have a profound effect on people's perceptions. Your nationality, cultural roots, and local customs impact your view of reality. These differences in perception influence the way you orient yourself to the world. For example, time is a reality all cultures readily acknowledge, but how they approach it can differ greatly.

To gain a clearer picture of what the world really looks like, you need to recognize the areas prone to your view of reality. In this topic, you will learn the differences found in cultural norms in relation to:

- time perception,
- codes of conduct,
- social orientation.

The first difference evident in cultural norms is the perception of time. Not everyone flows through time at the same pace. As Einstein observed, time is relative, even among different cultures. Some people relate to time as a recurring cycle, while others relate to time as a fleeting moment forever gone once it has transpired. In other words, people perceive time as either synchronous or sequential.

Because time is subjective, there is no right or wrong way to move through it. How you perceive and relate to time is more a matter of cultural convention than an imposed standard.

How do you perceive time? Do you relate to the past, present, and future as separate moments like footprints in the sand? Or is time for you a gray area in which the past, present, and future are more blurred, such as overlapping circles?

Behavioral distinctions
Sequential

Time is short. Once it's gone, it's lost forever. So don't put off until tomorrow what you can do today.

Synchronous

Those who are patient can reap great rewards, because timing is everything.

The second difference found in cultural norms is codes of conduct. Every group adopts rules and laws to regulate people's behavior. Seldom arbitrary, these codes can be ethical, legal, religious, governmental, even familial. As a member of your culture, you generally accept and abide by the agreed-upon rules. And members of other cultures do the same with the rules they create.

Ethical codes of conduct among cultures can vary significantly. What is considered appropriate in one society might be looked down upon in another. For instance, the binding power of decisions in a business setting might be different depending on whom you are working with.

Ethics of decision making
Anglo-Saxon/German

Anglo-Saxons and Germans view a decision that has been agreed upon orally as binding. They consider it ethically appropriate to stick to the agreement even if it has not been written into a contract.

Japanese

Ethically, Japanese associates have no problem backing out of an oral agreement. In fact, they perceive it as unethical to be bound to a decision when an unexpected turn of events makes their earlier choice appear unsound.

Who is right when it comes to acceptable codes of conduct? The answer is that it doesn't really matter; what does matter is that they are communicated and agreed upon by everyone.

The same answer can be applied to the third difference found in cultural norms: social orientation.

Every group relies on a social value system that dictates behavior, actions, and priorities. Some cultures place a strong emphasis on family and community, sometimes to the extent that it overshadows individual issues. Of course, there are cultures in which individual liberty is stressed and people are encouraged to be independent and pursue personal interests and goals.

Where does your social orientation lie? Consider three areas: personal priorities, business priorities, and family priorities.

If you had to rate them in order of importance, which area would you rate first? Why? Is there a potential conflict with your choices?

Example - Morgan is in sales, and Federico is in research and development for a medical instruments company. They met to discuss an upcoming trip.

Morgan: We're close to landing a big sale with that medical health services chain. We need to meet with its purchasing team in San Francisco next week, and I was hoping to have you join us.

Federico: Next week? I don't think I can make it. Sorry.

Morgan: I really need you there to answer the detailed questions the team members will probably ask.

Federico: My brother is getting married next week, and there's no way I can miss his wedding. Can you plan the trip for another time?

Morgan: This is going to be the biggest sale of the year. I had my parents coming into town next week, but they rescheduled when I told them about this. They totally understand. Won't your family feel the same way?

Federico: No, I don't think they would. This is a big event in our life and I can't miss it. I'm sorry. Can't you take John with you? He knows as much as I do.

Morgan: I'd rather have you. You know the instruments better than anyone. You know, if we land this account we'll exceed our projections for the entire year. It's imperative that you come, Federico.

Though many people consider their perceptions free from influence, cultural perceptions usually guide personal ones in areas such as time perception, codes of conduct, and social orientation. It's easier to understand other people when you're familiar with their perspective.

In this topic, you learned about the perceptual variations that exist with time perception, codes of conduct, and social orientation.

The correct use of nonverbal expression

There's a message with every movement. Do you know the message you're sending?

Psychological research of business communication has determined that while 80 percent to 90 percent of meeting time is devoted to verbal discussion, only 20 percent or less of the actual message is conveyed through the spoken word. That means up to 80 percent of the meaning is communicated by nonverbal elements. Just as spoken language varies by culture, so do the nonverbal elements of communication.

In this topic, you will examine modes of nonverbal communication and how they are used to express meaning in different cultures. Nonverbal cues are commonly expressed through gesticulation, facial expression, and body language.

The first mode of nonverbal communication is gesticulation. Gesticulation involves using gestures and signals to send messages. The use of gestures and signals can be a conscious or unconscious mode of communication on the part of the sender, and it is often very revealing.

How often have you seen a supervisor give the OK sign to express satisfaction with a job well done? Or perhaps a co-worker held his forefinger up to signify that you're "Number 1"?

These are classic examples of using gesticulations and gestures to express meaning nonverbally.

The second mode of nonverbal communication is facial expression. The face perhaps is the most telling nonverbal communicator, often more so than the spoken words. The eyes, the mouth, even the eyebrows, all provide clues to what the person is thinking and feeling. Have you ever encountered someone who tells you one thing but her face suggests another? A person might say she agrees with you, but she avoids making eye contact as she says it. Do you believe her?

The third mode of nonverbal communication is body language. This entails using the body's limbs and position to convey a message. The way a person uses her arms, legs, and posture during a conversation can accentuate or diminish the message she conveys. A person who pats you on the back or grabs your arm is also demonstrating body language.

For example, if an associate slouches in her chair with her head resting in one hand and tells you your idea is uninteresting, you could be inclined to believe it based on her body language.

Nonverbal messages communicate the sender's feelings about the subject being discussed. By recognizing the modes of nonverbal communication, you can gain a complete understanding of the intellectual and emotional message being sent.

But how do people from different cultures respond to these modes of communication? For example, is it appropriate to pat someone from Japan on the back?

Like any form of communication, the use of nonverbal expression can vary greatly depending on the culture you are interacting with. Nodding in agreement in one culture could literally mean the opposite in another. For this reason, it is critical to learn how nonverbal expression is interpreted in cultures different from your own.

The correct use of nonverbal communication begins with the culture. The distinction can be classified as expressive and nonexpressive cultures. If you are interacting with someone from an expressive culture, such as Latin, Middle Eastern, or African, you can expect a lot of nonverbal communication. By contrast, members of nonexpressive groups downplay the use of nonverbal expression. Japanese and Northern European cultures, such as Finland, fall into this category.

Example - nonverbal expressions.

Hand gestures

Using gestures and gesticulation is greatly encouraged within expressive cultures. It sends a message that you are engaged and interested.

Folded arms

Using broad gestures and gesticulations is discouraged within nonexpressive cultures. It is interpreted as overly dramatic and conveys unreliability and insincerity. The Japanese and Northern European cultures consider the use of gestures melodramatic.

Making eye contact

Members of expressive culture groups use their faces to great effect. For example, eye contact is important. The meaning behind this is that you are engaged and sincere, even if you are angry.

Avoiding eye contact

Avoid extensive eye contact with nonexpressive cultures. Members of these cultures consider excessive eye contact rude and disrespectful. It is taken to mean dominance and used to establish one's status.

Physical contact

Latin, Middle Eastern, and African cultures are quite comfortable making physical contact. Placing a hand on the shoulder or giving a pat on the back indicates friendship and acceptance.

Avoiding physical contact

Nonexpressive cultures use almost no forms of nonverbal communication. They keep their shoulders, legs, and arms still, and they avoid and discourage physical contact. However, they will sit with their legs crossed if they feel defensive.

Example - Cora is doing a presentation in front of a banking organization from Finland. If done well, the Finnish group will partner with Cora's financial institution to establish a presence in Helsinki

See each mode of nonverbal communication to find out how Cora made her presentation more effective.

Gestures

Cora found the team from Finland to be thoughtful and polite. She launched into her presentation with zeal and was sure to punctuate her statements with emphatic gestures to emphasize her point.

Eye contact

As the presentation continued, Cora was careful to avoid making too much eye contact with her hosts so as not to appear rude.

Defensive move

After she finished her presentation, Cora asked if there were any questions. A disagreement surfaced. She noticed several of her counterparts crossed their legs. Cora deftly de-emphasized the problem so they wouldn't feel defensive.

Based on the previous scenario, did Cora use nonverbal communication cues appropriately?

Not quite. Cora correctly avoided using eye contact with her Finnish colleagues. She knew that extended eye contact was interpreted as rude. Also, she wisely backed off on the disagreement after noticing her hosts crossing their legs. Cora knew that this was a subtle sign indicating defensiveness.

However, Cora would have been more effective if she had minimized her gesticulating. Excessive gesturing is seen as overly dramatic and possibly gave the Finnish team the perception that she was insincere and possibly unreliable.

Case Study: Question 1 of 2
Scenario

Edmund is working with bankers in Cameroon, an African nation bordering the Gulf of Guinea. He is there to help set up an investment arm of the local branch. Upon meeting his hosts, Edmund gave each member of the party pocket calculators as a gift. When they met to discuss the marketing strategy, he told a few jokes to make people feel more relaxed. As he discussed his ideas, Edmund felt free to use his hands to emphasize his points. However, he consciously avoided making eye contact so as not to make his associates think he was claiming a higher status. To make the point even stronger, he would occasionally pat various members on the back when they reached a decision that everyone felt comfortable with.

Determine whether Edmund's use of nonverbal expression was appropriate by answering the questions in order.

Question

Based on the scenario, was Edmund's use of nonverbal communication cues appropriate?

Options:

1. Yes, because he gestured often to make his points, avoided eye contact, and patted his colleagues on the back.

2. No, because he didn't make eye contact.

3. No, because he used his hands to express himself too often.

4. Yes, because he offered a gift, gestured often to make his points, avoided eye contact, and patted his colleagues on the back.

5. No, because he gestured often to make his points, avoided eye contact, and patted his colleagues on

the back.

Answer

Actually, Edmund would have been more effective if he had established and maintained eye contact.

Option 1: This is an incorrect choice. African cultures consider eye contact to be very important. It conveys sincerity and engagement. By avoiding eye contact, Edmund ignored a very important aspect of that culture.

Option 2: This choice is correct. While Edmund correctly used gestures and patted people on the back - important nonverbal cues in African cultures - he incorrectly avoided eye contact. African cultures consider eye contact to be very important.

Option 3: This choice is incorrect. The use of gestures is important and valued in African cultures. Gestures and eye contact send a message of being engaged and interested. Edmund did well by using expressive gestures but failed to make eye contact.

Option 4: This is an incorrect choice. Offering gifts is not an important form of expression in African culture. While gestures and patting colleagues' backs were in line with African culture, Edmund should have made eye contact, not avoided it.

Option 5: This choice is incorrect. The gesturing and back patting were appropriate because African cultures find those important. However, Edmund should have made eye contact, not avoided it, because in African culture it conveys sincerity and interest.

Case Study: Question 2 of 2

Scenario

Edmund is working with bankers in Cameroon, an African nation bordering the Gulf of Guinea. He is there to help set up an investment arm of the local branch. Upon meeting his hosts, Edmund gave each member of the party pocket calculators as a gift. When they met to discuss the marketing strategy, he told a few jokes to make people feel more relaxed. As he discussed his ideas, Edmund felt free to use his hands to emphasize his points. However, he consciously avoided making eye contact so as not to make his associates think he was claiming a higher status. To make the point even stronger, he would occasionally pat various members on the back when they reached a decision that everyone felt comfortable with.

Determine whether Edmund's use of nonverbal expression was appropriate by answering the questions in order.

Question

The approach Edmund took when he communicated nonverbally was directly related to the type of culture he interacted with. Identify distinctions Edmund considered when making his decisions. Match each expressiveness category to one or more appropriate cultures.

Options:

A. expressive culture
B. nonexpressive culture
Targets:
1. Northern European
2. African
3. Latin
4. Japanese
5. Middle Eastern
Answer
Actually, Latin, African, and Middle Eastern cultures traditionally appreciate and encourage nonverbal expression, and Japanese and Northern European cultures normally do not.

Since Northern Europeans tend to be nonexpressive, appropriate cues would be minimized gestures, less eye contact, and controlled body language. Edmund was in an expressive culture, so these would be inappropriate choices.

African culture is considered expressive, so large gestures, good eye contact, and expressive body language are accepted. Since Edmund was in an African culture, he made some overall good decisions based on these distinctions.

Latin, like African culture, is considered expressive, so large gestures, good eye contact, and expressive body language are accepted. Since Edmund was in an expressive culture, he made primarily good decisions based on these distinctions.

Since Japanese culture tends to be nonexpressive, appropriate cues would be minimized gestures, less eye contact and controlled body language. Edmund was in an expressive culture, so these would be inappropriate choices.

Middle Eastern, like African, culture is considered expressive, and they use large gestures, good eye contact, and clear body language. Since Edmund was in an expressive culture, he made predominantly good decisions based on these distinctions.

Communications style associated with content cultures

Whether it is an advertisement, a report, a stop sign, a tone of voice, or even the way a room is decorated, everything has a message.

Almost every expressed thought or action tells you something about the sender, and the receiver. The question is: Do you get the message?

Or, to put it more precisely, do you even look for the message? It depends on your preferred mode of communication. This preference for receiving messages can often be distinguished by the culture a person comes from. There are two prevailing approaches toward exchanging information, or sending and receiving messages: content and context. Content cultures prefer to put their information directly into the words and images they use to communicate.

The focus is on the information itself, rather than the circumstances that surround it. In other words, the substance of the information is independent of context such as relationships, environment, or other circumstances to convey meaning.

Content cultures include mainly Scandinavians and Germanic- and English-speaking cultures. In this topic, you will learn the communication style associated with content cultures. The communication style can be characterized as:

- literal,
- direct,
- expeditious.

The first characteristic indicative of a content culture's communication style is that it's literal. A literal approach can be described as precise, without embellishment. A content culture relies primarily on words and their exact definitions to convey meaning. Meaning is intended to be interpreted clearly and the margin of misunderstanding limited. In business communication, there is little use of metaphor, allusion, or subtlety.

In content cultures, a dialogue that insinuates or implies the meaning is rarely practiced. Members of a content culture depend on language that helps them get to the point.

This approach also results in a straightforward style, which is the second characteristic of a content culture's communication style: It is direct.

In a content culture, the shortest distance between two points is a straight line. The originator delivers the message directly to the intended recipient. Even when going through channels, the path of the message is as direct as the path allows. Although many factors and relationships go into the making of a decision, people from a content culture look to find the person who has the last word.

For example, a sales professional from a content culture will work his way through an organization's hierarchy and withhold key information until he speaks with the person who can make a decision.

The third characteristic of a content culture's communication style is that it is expeditious. The form a communication takes is usually dependent on what's most convenient and fits some external schedule. There is seldom much distinction made about which and what kind of information is e-mailed, faxed, sent by messenger, mailed, phoned, or delivered face to face except for the speed considered necessary and the need to suit the medium to the message format.

Gwen was working hard into the night. At 9:00 p.m., she needed some information from Vincent, a co- worker. She didn't hesitate to call him to discuss critical issues about the project. Together, they made significant decisions regarding a key project.

Example - see each factor to learn how Gwen's actions related to being expeditious.

Time

As long as Vincent was awake, Gwen didn't give much thought to what time of day a call is made.

Medium

Normally, important decisions are made in meetings, but Gwen didn't let that keep her from making one. Time was of the essence.

The message sent with a content culture's preferred mode of communication is simple: Business is business, so get to the point.

In this topic, you learned that the communication styles of content cultures can be characterized as literal, direct, and expeditious.

Determining the styles associated with context cultures

"Go ahead; make my day." - Clint Eastwood as policeman "Dirty" Harry Callahan in the 1983 film "Sudden Impact"

Eastwood's now-classic line is a perfect example of contextual communication. That is, the meaning of the words is almost entirely dependent on the situation that surrounds it, who is delivering the message, and the manner of the delivery--in this case, his character was holding a pointed gun and has a reputation as a policeman who shoots a lot of bad guys.

Societies that rely on the external circumstances that surround the spoken word include Asian, Middle Eastern, Mediterranean, Latin, and African cultures.

The factors used to enhance the meaning of the spoken word include location, ambiance, and the tone and status of the individual.

For context cultures, the words themselves often carry other meanings in a different context or situation. In this topic, you will learn the communication styles used by context cultures. The styles can be characterized as:

- nuanced,
- indirect,
- paced.

Consider the difference between a book and a film. In a book, the words are the sole source of information. But with a film, the message you receive comes from multiple sources. You have sights and sounds to consider. With all that information, the role words play in expressing a message changes. The result? A subtler, more implicit manner of communication that resonates off the surrounding circumstances

Example - see each characteristic to learn more about high-context communication styles.

Nuanced

High-context cultures rely on shared or common practices. Often a nuance involves a nonverbal cue or action that conveys implicit or understood information. Sometimes it involves a simple, vague statement that carries meaning to those within that cultural group only.

Indirect

High-context cultures believe in maintaining harmony. To avoid conflict, a person working with a member of a high-context group might use a more circuitous route to communicate a disagreement.

Paced

High-context cultures believe in establishing deep relationships. Conducting business in a slow, methodical manner allows for a relationship that is deeper and more trustful. The method is often just as important as the result.

George, a Westerner in Tokyo, walked into the meeting room prepared to address a disagreement that had surfaced. He found the chairs arranged in rows facing forward, like a classroom. Without a word being spoken, he understood the situation. Relationships among team members were not sufficiently developed yet for a public expression of opinion or debate. This was going to be an informational meeting to build rapport. Discussion of the challenged issue would take place later privately with his Japanese counterpart.

That was a lot of information for George to interpret from a roomful of empty chairs. But he'd been negotiating with the Japanese team for a few months and was becoming familiar with the nonverbal level of communication that existed in high-context cultures. Without a single word being spoken, all three communication styles blended together to send a clear message. Consider the layout of the room. Normally, a conference room would have chairs situated around the table, which suggests an open discussion.

The nuance of placing chairs classroom style meant the focus would center on information gathering rather than open discussion. The arrangement indirectly conveyed the desire to handle the matter privately, and the delay of making a decision set the pace for the process.

Context cultures place a great deal of value on behavior that promotes harmony and understanding. Nuance, indirectness, and pacing allow people in context cultures to move a group smoothly forward until the relationship is established and a decision can be made.

Now that you understand the communication styles practiced by high-context cultures, how can you recognize it in cultures you aren't familiar with?

Many professionals from high-content groups need to get used to identifying the way business is conducted in high-context cultures. Content-oriented groups conduct business as a task-oriented process that focuses on making decisions in a swift and efficient manner. This is not always the case with high-context groups.

Example - see each action to learn a clue that will help you recognize the characteristic.

Recognizing nuance

You can recognize nuanced behavior by listening for vague phrases such as, "This is important." The degree of importance might be understood only by the group. Seek clarity when that occurs. Also match nuanced actions, such as allowing senior citizens to enter a room first.

Recognizing indirectness

Be aware of indirect communication when there is a disagreement. Sometimes it is a generic response that seems like there is in fact an agreement. Sometimes indirect behavior is expressed through simple silence. Again, ask questions to gain clarity.

Recognizing pace

It is wise to be aware of the importance of relationship building and its vital component: trust. Observe the situation to find out if people avoid making decisions or if your direct question is countered with a rapport-building question. Allow your counterparts to proceed at their pace.

Graham works at a telecommunications firm in England. He is in Thailand to piece together a deal to install pay phones throughout the country. The Thai representatives are hospitable and things seem to be going well.

Example - See each phone call to learn how Graham was flexible to the context culture's communication styles.

Phone 1

Graham felt like he was making progress when the senior member told him that getting the proposal processed was an urgent matter. Satisfied that he was getting through, Graham moved on to other issues.

Phone 2

When an issue regarding the price of installation arose, the members of the team seemed unable to understand Graham's English. Graham decided to discuss the issue with the senior manager at another time.

Phone 3

Graham asked if the senior manager was in a position to make a decision. The senior manager replied by asking him how many children he had. Graham smiled and said he was the proud father of three girls.

Based on the way Graham reacted to the team's behavior, do you think he recognized the high-context communication styles?

Graham recognized the team's inability to understand him as an indirect response to the conflict surrounding the price of installation. He also recognized the senior member's rapport-building question as an indicator that the pace of the proceedings had not yet reached the decision-making stage. However, he should have clarified what the senior manager meant when he said the proposal was an urgent matter. Would it be completed next week? He didn't recognize the nuance involved with such a broad statement.

Learning aid - **Content Culture Traits**

Content Cultures	Communication Styles	Work Habits
Americans	Unemotional	Plan ahead meticulously
Australians	Direct	Take a linear approach to tasks
Austrians	Strive for precision	Time conscious
British	Use logic to make points	Subdivide projects
Canadians	Prefer succinct, to-the-point language	Delegate authority
Germans	Intent on making a decision	Rely on empirical data for making decisions
New Zealanders		
Scandinavians	Action oriented	Follow guidelines
South Africans	Rarely interrupt	Punctual
Swiss		Prefer fixed agendas

Learning Aid - Context Culture Traits

Building Better Work Relationships

Context Cultures	Communication Styles	Work Habits
Africans	Nuanced	Multitask
Arabians	Indirect	Delegate to relatives
Central Americans	Paced	Flexing timetables
	Relationship focused	Rely on oral information
Indians	Extroverted	
Italians	Interweave professional and social	
Middle Eastern		
Portuguese	Gregarious	
Russians		
South Americans		
Spanish		
Chinese	Nuanced	Methodical
Japanese	Indirect	Rely on procedures
Singaporeans	Paced	Make decisions by consensus
Taiwanese	Introverted	Plan slowly
Turkish	Patient	Rely on facts
	Unemotional	
	Listeners	

Customs and Etiquette

"Manners are of more importance than laws. Manners are what vex or soothe, corrupt or purify, exalt or debase, barbarize or refine us, by a constant, steady, uniform, insensible operation, like that of the air we breathe in." -- Edmund Burke, British statesman

British statesman Burke understood the importance of this often-overlooked element of communication. You might not think of customs and etiquette as forms of communication, but they are, and ones that vary widely among cultures.

A crown, ceremonial robes, an expensive suit: What do these things have in common?

They are a few of the many different trappings associated with status. Status is not ordained by the same route in every culture, nor is it proclaimed by the same symbols. In business, you need to know whom you are dealing with. Status might be hierarchical, professional, consensual, experiential, genetic, informational, educational, chronological, or simply nominal, but it is often some combination of these.

"Courtesy is the one coin you can never have too much of or be stingy with." --John Wanamaker, merchant

Good manners are more than just a superficial display of courtesy. For many cultures, manners represent significant underlying cultural customs or values. Disregarding or overlooking some kinds of socially expected manners can be interpreted as a severe insult, from which it is almost impossible to recover a relationship.

Cultural variations in customs and etiquette

"Manners are of more importance than laws. Manners are what vex or soothe, corrupt or purify, exalt or debase, barbarize or refine us, by a constant, steady, uniform, insensible operation, like that of the air we breathe in." -- Edmund Burke, British statesman

British statesman Burke understood the importance of this often-overlooked element of communication. You might not think of customs and etiquette as forms of communication, but they are, and ones that vary widely among cultures.

Culturewide etiquette displays a large number of assumptions a culture holds about itself and its values. Even when there are language barriers, understanding and observing etiquette formalities holds significant value. It can.

- establish a basis for communication,
- enable you to exhibit appropriate respect,
- make people more relaxed and open in business or social settings,

- help prevent misunderstandings.

If you will be doing business, whether at home or abroad, with people from different cultural backgrounds, it is important to understand how their manners and customs may vary from accustomed ones. The topics in this lesson will introduce you to some of the common variations in cultural customs that you would be likely to encounter in an intercultural business relationship.

Ways in which status is conferred

A crown, ceremonial robes, an expensive suit: What do these things have in common?

They are a few of the many different trappings associated with status. Status is not ordained by the same route in every culture, nor is it proclaimed by the same symbols. In business, you need to know whom you are dealing with. Status might be hierarchical, professional, consensual, experiential, genetic, informational, educational, chronological, or simply nominal, but it is often some combination of these.

The form of the status can affect how much competition exists, whether decisions are made consensually or unilaterally. Status also reflects in responsibility.

There are varying types of status. In this topic, you will learn to recognize:

- attributed status,
- acquired status,
- nominal status.

The first type of status is attributed status. Attributed status is conferred by general agreement because of some inherent trait or characteristic the person possesses.

For example, a person can gain attributed status by virtue of advanced age or by family name.

The second type of status is acquired status. Acquired status is achieved in some way, perhaps through obtaining academic degrees, experience, or promotions. Acquired status is based more on meritocracy; the person with status earned it.

For example, a lawyer who has argued many civil action suits involving water rights may have earned the status of an expert in that field by virtue of his experience.

The third type of status is nominal status. Although nominal status--status in name only--invests no authority or responsibility in the status holder, the status still commands a modicum of respect. Examples of nominal status include:

- ceremonial positions, such as a grand marshal of a parade,
- assigned titles, such as knightship,
- associated titles, such as the United States president also being the commander in chief.

The objective and relative status of the parties you interact with in a business setting have a major effect on the business relationship that can be sought or achieved. In order to make the most of your relationships, familiarize yourself with how status has been conferred, that is, whether it is attributed, acquired, or nominal.

Guidelines for appropriate cultural manners

Sorin Dumitrascu

"Courtesy is the one coin you can never have too much of or be stingy with." --John Wanamaker, merchant

Good manners are more than just a superficial display of courtesy. For many cultures, manners represent significant underlying cultural customs or values. Disregarding or overlooking some kinds of socially expected manners can be interpreted as a severe insult, from which it is almost impossible to recover a relationship.

Sincere good manners are a way of showing sincere respect. In this topic, you will learn three general rules that constitute common courtesy. When interacting with different cultures, you should:

- respect personal distance,
- match dining etiquette,
- honor taboos.

The first rule of good manners is to respect personal distance. Allowing for individual variations, each culture and nationality has a generally accepted attitude about how much personal distance each person requires between himself and another person.

It's a social buffer of space that surrounds each individual. Approaching someone closer than his buffer zone makes him feel uncomfortable.

The second rule of good manners is to match dining etiquette. Sharing a meal is probably the most common social activity associated with business relationships in any culture. The meal might be in a restaurant, at a large reception or gathering, or in someone's home. Because dining is a universal and frequent activity, every culture has a large number of rituals and generally acknowledged etiquette that is specific to dining.

Dining etiquette can include what apparel is worn or not worn, such as shoes, ties, and jackets. Etiquette can also include what the standard seating arrangements are; how to politely handle the food, whether it's with eating implements or with hands; and how to display appreciation of a meal. These customs vary widely from culture to culture.

Example - see each location to learn about a few customs from around the world.

Ivory Coast

In the Ivory Coast, you are expected to arrive 15 minutes late to a dinner party. You are expected to remain silent when dining and to use the right hand only.

Poland

In Poland, expect the host to make a toast on your behalf. It is then up to you to make a toast to him in return. Also, it is considered rude to leave a dinner party early.

Denmark

If you are dining in Denmark, it is customary for the person sitting to the left of the hostess to offer a toast to her during dessert.

Philippines

In the Philippines, it is polite to appear reluctant to go to the dinner table once the host has announced that dinner is served.

Because there are so many variations, it is not unusual to find that good dining etiquette in one culture is perceived as bad manners, or even insulting behavior, in another.

The third rule of good manners is to honor taboos. Most cultures have both explicit and implicit behavioral taboos.

A taboo is any behavior that is considered completely unacceptable for either social or religious reasons.

Every culture has its own taboos. For example, in Madagascar, eggs may not be passed directly to others. In Russia, you should never ask anyone of the opposite gender where the bathroom is.

Example - see each location to learn more about behavioral taboos.

Malaysia

It is taboo in Malaysia to point with your index finger.

Arab countries

In Arab countries, displaying the sole of your shoe is an insult.

Even in one culture, the types of situations that require a display of good manners can be vast. But respecting personal distance, matching dining etiquette, and honoring taboos can carry you through the majority of face-to-face intercultural business interactions.

But how can you make the right choice?

Unless you are intimately familiar with a culture, it is often impossible to know what the customs are without being told. In order to respect personal space, match dining etiquette, and honor taboos, always:

- observe and mimic group actions and behavior,
- avoid initiating actions and behavior,
- take cues from the person you are interacting with.

When in a cultural situation in which you are not familiar with the expected etiquette, you need to be attentive. Observe the behavior of those around you, and mimic the necessary manners. When do people sit at a table to eat? Do they talk? What do they talk about?

Avoid initiating any actions or conversations to prevent yourself from saying or doing anything that might be considered rude or insulting.

When interacting with one person, take your cues from his response. Be careful here. Often a person from a different culture will not directly reprimand you when you broach a custom or taboo. He may become silent or change the subject.

Example - Rosa was in India doing business with a pharmaceutical firm. Seema, her contact, invited her to a dinner party. Rosa informed Seema that she would wear a short skirt she bought for the trip. Seema smiled and asked her about her family.

How did Rosa do? Did she follow the guidelines and behave in an appropriate manner for her Indian hosts? See each situation to learn more about Rosa's behavior.

Passing food

At the dinner party, Rosa was careful to pass food to other guests with her left hand like everyone else.

Personal space

Rosa noticed Seema kept a fair physical distance between herself and the people she spoke with. Rosa did the same.

Rosa was smart to mimic the behavior of her hostess, Seema. When she saw her maintaining a fair distance from other guests, she wisely did the same. She also astutely noticed that the guests passed food with their left hand only. She simply complied. However, she might have noticed that Seema didn't react well to the thought of her wearing a short skirt, which is not acceptable in India. It would have been appropriate for her to honor that taboo.

Case Study: Question 1 of 2
Scenario

Drew was in the Czech Republic working with a bank to create a software networking program. His contact was Jiri. Before the meeting, he noticed Jiri in a meeting with his associates. Though there were only a few of them seated in the room, they were spread out enough to take up most of the large conference table. After the meeting Jiri shook hands with Drew. and promptly offered his card. Drew was glad to see it was printed in English. Drew offered his card with his information printed in English and in Czech. Once in the conference room, Jiri sat down at the large table. Drew took a seat across from Jiri so he could interact face to face. That evening at a dinner party Jiri had, Drew waited along with the group until the oldest woman had been served. The conversation at the dinner table was lively. The main topics were family and music. Intrigued by this culture and country, Drew mentioned how hard it must have been to live under Communist rule. Jiri and the group reacted with polite silence. Drew replied sincerely that it must have been a trying time.

Answer the following questions in order.

Question

Based on the scenario, did Drew effectively follow the guidelines for appropriate behavior?

Options:

1. No, because he initiated the conversation surrounding the era of Communist rule and continued despite Jiri's cue not to.

2. Yes, because he observed and mimicked group behavior concerning personal distance and table manners, and he initiated a topic of conversation.

3. No, because he mimicked group behavior concerning personal distance and table manners.

Answer

Actually, Drew should have avoided initiating a conversation and heeded Jiri's cue, thus honoring this taboo.

Option 1: This is the correct choice. Drew should have taken cues directly from Jiri on acceptable topics of conversation. Drew should have noted what others were discussing, and stuck to those topics. By initiating talk on a taboo topic, he showed disrespect.

Option 2: This is an incorrect choice. By initiating a topic of discussion, Drew mistakenly chose a taboo topic that silenced the group. He should have followed the topics that others initiated. Drew did do well with following other customs and behaviors.

Option 3: This is an incorrect choice. While Drew did correctly mimic behavior on dinner etiquette and personal distance, he initiated a topic of conversation, which turned out to be taboo. Drew should have followed the topics initiated by others.

Case Study: Question 2 of 2

Scenario

Drew was in the Czech Republic working with a bank to create a software networking program. His contact was Jiri. Before the meeting, he noticed Jiri in a meeting with his associates. Though there were only a few of them seated in the room, they were spread out enough to take up most of the large conference table. After the meeting

Jiri shook hands with Drew. and promptly offered his card. Drew was glad to see it was printed in English. Drew offered his card with his information printed in English and in Czech. Once in the conference room, Jiri sat down at the large table. Drew took a seat across from Jiri so he could interact face to face. That evening at a dinner party Jiri had, Drew waited along with the group until the oldest woman had been served. The conversation at the dinner table was lively. The main topics were family and music. Intrigued by this culture and country, Drew mentioned how hard it must have been to live under Communist rule. Jiri and the group reacted with polite silence. Drew replied sincerely that it must have been a trying time.

Answer the following questions in order.

Question

What were the guidelines you used to determine whether Drew behaved appropriately in a different culture?

Options:

1. Observe and mimic group actions and behavior.
2. Avoid initiating actions and behavior.
3. Take cues from the person you are interacting with.
4. Inform others of your cultural preferences.
5. Use your instinct.

Answer

Actually, when interacting with people from a culture you know little about, observe and mimic group behavior, avoid initiating actions and behavior, and take cues from the person you are speaking with.

Option 1: You used this guideline to analyze Drew's behavior and determined that he did not behave appropriately. Had he been observant, he would have noticed that the main topics of conversation were family and music, not politics.

Option 2: This choice is correct. By using this guideline to determine whether Drew's actions were proper, you noticed that he initiated a conversation--and on a taboo subject. This was not appropriate behavior in this situation.

Option 3: You used this guideline to help you determine that Drew's actions were not appropriate in this situation. After he initiated the political conversation, he did not notice that Jiri and the group fell silent; instead, he continued the conversation.

Option 4: This is an incorrect choice. This is not one of the guideline you would use to determine whether Drew behaved appropriately. In fact, it might demonstrate that he emphasized his culture over the one he is visiting, which is disrespectful.

Option 5: This choice is incorrect. Using your instinct is not a guideline for analyzing Drew's behavior because it is too subjective. The guidelines you should use are much more objective and rely on observation and simple rules.

Each culture adheres to its own set of manners and taboos. The message behind practicing good manners is respect. And good manners only are effective if they are done with sincerity. This practice will go far in establishing a good intercultural relationship.

In this topic, you learned how to respect personal distance, match dining etiquette, and honor taboos.

As the global marketplace evolves, you will become increasingly aware that it is indeed a small world. But with that discovery, you might learn that it is a fascinating world too. You can enrich your business relationships by embracing and respecting the differences that make people so interesting. And as you expand your cultural horizons, you might find your personal life enriched as well.

Learning aid - **Cultural Etiquette**

Cultures	Dinner Etiquette	Taboos
Botswana	Wait for your host to seat you. Eat with your right hand only.	Avoid political discussions.
China	Don't drink wine until the host invites you. Be prepared for the host to ask you to sing a song (in your language).	Avoid public displays of affection. Don't talk about the government.
France	If you are offered a drink before dinner, rise to accept it. Keep both hands on the table.	Avoid asking questions about one's personal life.
Germany	Eat everything on your plate.	Don't keep your hands in your pockets.
Japan	Don't begin to eat until seniors do.	Avoid physical contact.
Spain	Always show up 15 to 20 minutes late for a dinner party. Never swear.	The American "OK" hand sign is considered an offensive gesture.

CHAPTER FOUR

Effective Intergender Relationships

His and Hers

You like potato and I like potahto, You like tomato and I like tomahto; Potato, potahto, tomato, tomahto! Let's call the whole thing off!" --Ira Gershwin, "Let's Call the Whole Thing Off!"

No one questions that men and women are different. The differences make the world go around. But some of those differences are more perceived than real. A lot of who you are and how you act as an adult has to do with how you were raised, and most girls are raised differently from the way in which boys are raised.

If, from the age of 2 to the age of 18, you received a dollar every time you nodded your head, what would be the result?

You would be a millionaire who walked around with a bobbing head the rest of your life. Much of the masculine or feminine behavior you exhibit as an adult is not innate to your gender. It's actually a group of habits that you acquired as a child.

"It's a guy thing."

When behavior is categorized as a "guy thing," both men and women smile knowingly, but their understanding of the phrase stems from different sources. Men mean that the significance is "beyond the understanding" of women, like an inside joke which is only understood by the members of a certain group or, in this case, gender. Women mean that it's a type of "silliness" exclusive to men.

"That's girl talk."

Women and men agree that "girl talk" is about relationships and events: Who did what to whom, and why? This is the stuff of life to most women, and a lot of men regard it as trivial. Girl talk doesn't solve any problems or fix anything, so what's the point?

Would you use only one wrench to tighten all styles and sizes of bolts? Probably not. You'd use the right tool for the job. The same is true of using the right communication style for a given situation.

Women's and men's communication styles each have a lot to offer, but just like some tools, not all aspects of either style are appropriate or effective for all situations.

Men and women communicate differently

You like potato and I like potahto, You like tomato and I like tomahto; Potato, potahto, tomato, tomahto! Let's call the whole thing off!" --Ira Gershwin, "Let's Call the Whole Thing Off!"

No one questions that men and women are different. The differences make the world go around. But some of those differences are more perceived than real. A lot of who you are and how you act as an adult has to do with how you were raised, and most girls are raised differently from the way in which boys are raised.

And it's not just how your parents treated you.

The entire world you grew up in is structured to treat boys and girls in different ways. And all those influences, from television to music to schooling to advertising, formed you into acting in the feminine or masculine way you do.

Although the differences in male and female communication patterns may be occasionally charming in social interactions, the confusion generated by the differences can cause a lot of problems in work interactions.

Interactions

Generally, women are nurturing and men tend to be unemotional; men show their anger and women are conciliatory; men slap each other on the back and women hug.

Learned habits

Although these are familiar styles of communication for each gender, the behaviors are not innate. They're learned habits, not inborn functions of gender.

At work, you need all your relationships to be productive. The confusion that arises because of the differences in the way women and men communicate wastes a lot of time and productivity. If you can understand the differences, you can interpret and adapt.

The topics in this lesson provide background information that will help you develop more adaptive intergender communication skills. You'll learn about:

• factors affecting gender communication styles,

- communication differences between men and women,
- techniques for communicating with the opposite gender.

Developmental factors that influence communication

If, from the age of 2 to the age of 18, you received a dollar every time you nodded your head, what would be the result?

You would be a millionaire who walked around with a bobbing head the rest of your life. Much of the masculine or feminine behavior you exhibit as an adult is not innate to your gender. It's actually a group of habits that you acquired as a child.

You probably don't even realize it because almost everyone else of your gender behaves the same way.

These communication habits form as a result of developmental factors that influence the ways in which men and women communicate. The factors are:

- genetics,
- gender-role modeling,
- socialization.

Whether you start life with an XX (female) or an XY (male) chromosome probably has the most profound influence on who you are. The genetic factor is the primary distinction between men and women. The biological, anatomical, and hormonal makeup of your gender certainly influences behavior.

Genetics

In communication, genetics account for a woman's higher-pitched voice and a man's more physically assertive presence.

Personality

Although genetics determine a lot of your personality, most of the way you communicate is learned, not predetermined by your chromosomes.

After genetics, the second factor that influences communication behavior is gender-role modeling. One way children learn is by mimicking behavior. And if it's appropriate behavior, children receive a reward for it. The reward might be a smile or a hug or parental approval.

Example

Boy

Boys receive approval for acting like their fathers or like "little men." Likewise, a boy could be chastised for crying. After all, his father probably tends to be stoic, not emotional.

Girl

Girls receive approval for acting like their mothers-- sweet or nurturing. Similarly, a girl might be reprimanded for being too loud. Her mother is probably demure and not aggressive.

Parental reward

Kids learn quickly that they will receive a reward for acting more like one parent than the other, and parents treat children differently depending on whether they are boys or girls.

Parental approval

For a child, parental approval is a form of love, and if behaving like one parent or the other brings approval, then the child will quickly learn to behave that way.

Think about the gender-role modeling in your life. What effect has it had? Do you see any communication behaviors that you retain from childhood? Take a minute to jot your insights down on a piece of paper.

As children get older and interact with more people in school and play, the gender-role modeling they receive from their parents is reinforced by the rest of the world around them. That's the socialization process, which is the third factor that influences how men and women communicate. Socialization can come from friends at school, the media, or other adults who play a role in a child's life, such as a coach or a teacher.

The world is full of dual messages about how women and men behave, from "Pink is for girls; blue is for boys" to dolls or trucks, skirts or pants, makeup or mustaches. Boys are seldom told to smile for no reason, and girls are rarely told to defend themselves.

To understand why men and women communicate in such different manners, you need to understand that men and women were "trained" differently as children. Women weren't born nodding and discussing relationships, and men weren't born interrupting and talking about sports. Although genetics influence behavior, the majority of the communication behaviors associated with gender are the result of gender-role modeling and socialization.

Typical communication styles used by men
"It's a guy thing."

When behavior is categorized as a "guy thing," both men and women smile knowingly, but their understanding of the phrase stems from different sources. Men mean that the significance is "beyond the understanding" of women, like an inside joke which is only understood by the members of a certain group or, in this case, gender.

Women mean that it's a type of "silliness" exclusive to men.

The different meanings attributed to the same phrase provide a vivid illustration of the differences in the way men and women communicate. Neither men's nor women's communications styles are right or wrong; they're just different.

Men's communication styles tend to be focused around actions--doing and thinking--whereas women's communication styles are usually focused on understanding and feeling. Specifically, most men's communication styles are:

• goal-oriented • competitive

• active

• analytical.

The most prominent aspect of the communication style of most men is that it is goal-oriented. Men speak with purpose, often to resolve or fix a perceived problem. Men focus their conversation on solutions. Because the goal is to solve, they tend to speak literally and concretely.

In addition to being goal-oriented, many men have a competitive communication style. Men speak to their own self-interest in sweeping, categorical statements that make them sound confident and persuasive. They want to score conversational points. They often interrupt other speakers in an effort to control or dominate.

Example - see each instance of Jim for more information.

Jim 1

"I don't talk for the sake of talking. I like to get to the point and accomplish something in my conversations. I like to provide solutions to problems, not just talk."

Jim 2

"I come across as strong and confident, and I have no problem interrupting to make my point. Winners succeed, and winning is my middle name."

The third aspect of the communication style of men is that it's active. Active communication involves using active verbs rather than passive verbs. It also means using strong, assertive language.

Sam blasted his way through that report.

A passive version would be "The report was completed by Sam in a fairly short time." The active version uses the word "blasted," which is a strong, active verb.

I'm interested in the new job position.

A passive version would be "The new job position is interesting." In the active version, the emphasis is on the speaker, not the job.

I'll win the sales contest.

A weak version would be "I plan on winning the sales contest." Men tend to use assertive language that clearly states their intention.

You're wrong.

A weak version would be "I think that maybe you're incorrect." Men tend to say what they think without being too concerned about the feelings involved.

Men prefer verbs in the active tense and use an assertive or forceful vocabulary that shows self-confidence.

Finally, most men have an **analytical** communication style. Men like to exhibit their independent thinking rather than express their emotions. They focus on how and why something happens, not on how they feel about it.

Analytical communication involves words that imply analysis, such as "think," "assume," "consider," "why," and "because." Examples of analytical communication include:

- I think the solution is to trim the size of the team.
- We're over budget because of the extra traveling.
- If you stop to think about it, you'll see the answer.

Although men's communication styles are clear and constructive in many situations, the intent is not always perceived as warm or friendly by women. When communicating with women, men should consider making their communication styles less forceful. What other men may see as comradely competition, women may see as personal affront.

As you communicate with men, remember that in general, they have a communication style that is goal-oriented, competitive, active, and analytical.

Typical communication styles used by women

"That's girl talk."

Women and men agree that "girl talk" is about relationships and events: Who did what to whom, and why? This is the stuff of life to most women, and a lot of men regard it as trivial. Girl talk doesn't solve any problems or fix anything, so what's the point?

The different significance attached to girl talk is a prime example of the difference in men's and women's communication style. Women want to understand the world; men want to fix it.

Women, in general, use communication styles that help build rapport and understanding. Relationships are the key for women in communication.

Example - see each type for more information on women's communication styles.

Process-oriented

One of the most prominent aspects of a woman's communication style is that it's process- oriented. Women converse to understand themselves, other people, and the world around them. They ask questions as they seek to know, not seek to control.

Conciliatory

In addition to being process-oriented, women have a conciliatory communication style. Women seek workable compromises and win-win situations. They are more apt to share power than to wield it unilaterally.

Indirect

In an effort to not offend, women often communicate using an indirect style. Women use qualifiers such as "might" or "would." They also tend to end a sentence with a tag question, such as "OK?"

Relational

Finally, women often have a relational communication style that expresses understanding, nurturing, and empathy. Phrases such as "I understand" and "I know how you feel" demonstrate the relational style.

Explore examples of process-oriented, conciliatory, indirect, and relational styles by selecting each example in turn. Use a piece of paper to jot down what style you think is being demonstrated in each of the numbered images.

Example 1

"I understand what you're talking about. Sometimes these projects are difficult to manage. I certainly empathize with your concerns about how this will develop."

Example 2

"Can you tell me more about why you're upset over the funding changes? I'd like to have a better understanding of your concerns and how this whole approach will evolve."

Example 3

"I might be able to get the report done by this Friday. I'll probably need to talk with you later in the week about my progress, OK?"

Example 4

"I'd really like to find a win-win solution for this problem. I'd be glad to share the responsibilities with you. It's not necessary for me to be the sole leader on this project."

Compare what you wrote down with the actual styles the woman on the previous page was demonstrating. In example 1, she was relational; in example 2, process-oriented; in example 3, indirect; and in example 4, conciliatory.

How did you do? Were you on track? Learning about women's communication styles is fundamental to your success in communicating with women.

Although the communication style used by most women is caring and supportive in many situations, its intent is frequently misinterpreted by men. Women who employ more directness can avoid some of the intergender communication issues.

Remember, women tend to be process-oriented, conciliatory, indirect, and relational in their communication, which helps them realize their goal of understanding others and building rapport.

Effective feminine or masculine communication techniques in a conversational situation

Would you use only one wrench to tighten all styles and sizes of bolts? Probably not. You'd use the right tool for the job. The same is true of using the right communication style for a given situation.

Women's and men's communication styles each have a lot to offer, but just like some tools, not all aspects of either style are appropriate or effective for all situations.

You'll find that expanding your style repertoire can help you make your point more clearly so others-- especially those of the opposite gender - will understand it better.

In general, men and women take a very different approach to communication. Men tend to focus on doing, and women tend to focus on relationships.

Men

"In our communication styles, we tend to be goal-oriented, analytical, and competitive, and we tend to use action-oriented language. We solve problems and take action.

Women

"In our communication, we tend to be process-oriented, conciliatory, indirect, and relational. We want to understand others and build rapport."

Many common business situations are best facilitated by using a particular communication style, even if that style is not inherent to your gender. These situations are:

- establishing or building relationships through connection,
- handling "stuck" or deadlocked communications with conciliation,
- making your point or stimulating action with assertiveness,
- determining what's happening, or what to do, with analysis.

Connection is a technique that is part of the process-oriented communication style favored by women. It's particularly effective when starting to work with new people or a new situation. By connecting, you build rapport, which is essential for productive relationships. If others seem hesitant or closed, ask them how they feel about the situation. If they talk about their feelings, share your own feelings.

As a project planner, Andy met with many engineers at his company. He would always express his understanding as they talked about tight project schedules. He usually asked the engineers how they were doing and how they felt as a way of keeping communication open.

Not all situations need to be win/lose. Sometimes the best approach is conciliation. Conciliation can be best achieved by compromising or cooperating. Conciliation is applicable to any situation in which there are differences of opinion and it appears that you're in a deadlock.

Example

Compromise

Barry and his controller disagreed on how some expense charges should be allocated. Barry compromised and charged half the expenses to his department.

Cooperate

Barry's production leader was arguing with him about procedures. Barry suggested they cooperate so they'd both receive benefits from the agreement.

Some situations are best served by using assertiveness. When stating a viewpoint, directing a team, or debating a difference of opinion, being assertive will add force to your delivery. The keys to being assertive are:
• using strong action verbs
• avoiding hesitant, passive language.

If you want to make a point, use strong words. Telling a team member that she did an "outstanding" job is more powerful than saying she did a "nice" job. Also, avoid using hesitant words such as "might," "maybe," and "probably" when stating what you'll do. Instead of "I'll probably get the report done," use more assertive language, such as "I'll finish the report by noon." This shows your commitment.

Julie was impressed with the proposal that Beth, her assistant, had written. Julie met with Beth and told her that her writing was masterful. When Beth left the meeting, she was beaming.

Some situations require more of a mental or an intellectual approach than an emotional approach. Confusion or a need for clearer understanding is the signal for using analysis skills, a common male communication style. You can use specific key words to help catalyze analysis in these situations. Words such as "think," "assume," "consider," "why," and "because" are all associated with the analytical process. By asking yourself and others to think about the situation, you'll help everyone be more productive.

Tara was concerned about the new design process. It seemed inefficient to her. She told Tim, who developed the process, that she thought the second step was too complex. She asked him to think about ways it could be shortened. A few days later, Tim presented a new process that was significantly more effective.

Selecting the right communication technique is a judgment call that you make according to your situation and desired outcome. You need to observe the circumstances and use your common sense to decide what's most appropriate.

The styles of connection, conciliation, assertiveness, and analysis actually represent an array of communication tools that can be applied according to the circumstances or situation.

Toward Gender Dexterity

Communication between genders often resembles the telephone game. The recipient often hears a message that has only the barest resemblance to what the sender originally intended.

The vast majority of readers would assume that the first statement on the preceding page was made by a man and the second by a woman. Men and women have different delivery styles in:

- content, or what is being verbally delivered,

- structure, or how the content is being delivered.

What's wrong with these statements? "All men enjoy sports." "All women want children."

The problem is that not all men think or behave alike. Neither do all women. You can probably point to at least one person of the opposite gender with whom you have more in common than you do with some of the members of your own gender. A less-discussed problem is that men and women often stereotype members of their own gender. Dealing with people according to group membership is a tempting shortcut around getting to know them as individuals.

There will always be two genders, and for the conceivable future, they'll have to work together. Ignoring differences in communication styles only perpetuates problems. The best solution in the workplace is for each gender to give a little. That means men and women need to incorporate the most effective communication elements of each gender. The SAVE model will help you keep talking with the opposite gender.

Developing skills to communicate better with the opposite gender

In the children's game of "Telephone," a message is whispered from child to child, and the last one has to say aloud what she thinks the message is. It's funny because the message is usually garbled in transmission and seldom resembles the original by the time it reaches the last person in the row.

Communication between genders often resembles the telephone game. The recipient often hears a message that has only the barest resemblance to what the sender originally intended.

You can use several strategies to help clear up the static that occurs when women and men communicate. As with many problems, it helps to understand the underlying causes before you start applying solutions.

The causes of intergender miscommunication are a result of communication style differences as well as preconceptions men and women have about each other. Developing better intergender communication skills can result in:

- improved communication with the opposite gender,
- increased respect for other points of view,
- more productive work relationships.

Probably nothing will ever entirely demystify all the differences between men and women, but eliminating some of the confusion from their communication will allow them to work together more productively and with more satisfaction.

The topics in this lesson offer additional insight into real and perceived communication differences between men and women and provide some specific suggestions for improvement.

Gender-specific delivery styles

"How about that new ball team?"

"Is that a new hair style?"

The vast majority of readers would assume that the first statement on the preceding page was made by a man and the second by a woman. Men and women have different delivery styles in:

- content, or what is being verbally delivered,
- structure, or how the content is being delivered.

Generally speaking, men and women tend to talk about different content areas. It's no surprise that men talk about sports, money, and business, and women talk about people, feelings, and relationships. The only topic that researchers find women and men addressing equally is sex, but even then, men often approach it from a sport perspective and women from a relational one. You gain dexterity in your intergender communications by understanding what each gender tends to talk about.

Structure refers to how content is delivered. In general, men structure communication to be precise and to the point. They tend to avoid long explanations and overuse of adjectives. If you ask a man about a successful meeting, he'll most likely say that "it was great."

Women tend to structure communication that is descriptive, apologetic, and vague. If you ask a woman about a successful meeting, you'll get a good idea of everything that occurred and how everyone felt.

Example - Look for content and structure differences as Stuart and Tina talked about changes at their company.

Tina: I just can't believe that we're laying off almost 10 percent of the company. This is disastrous. I feel so bad for everyone, don't you?

Stuart: Hey, that's life. Sometimes you win, and sometimes you lose. They'll do fine.

Tina: But what about our department? We have so many good people. I'd really miss anyone who was let go. We're almost like a family. I'm as close to some of our team members as I am my own sisters.

Stuart: Maybe, but the company needs to survive. It's that simple. Business is like sports. If you have the right players and make the right plays, you'll win. That's what it's all about.

Tina: That view seems awfully callous to me. We're real people with real families and lives. How can you be so insensitive?

Stuart: I'm not insensitive, just realistic. I know it'll be hard for some, but it's the best we can do, considering the situation.

Tina: Well, I suppose so, but I still can't help feeling sorry for some of the employees. They put a lot of years into this place and just lost those years overnight. It's disheartening.

Tina and Stuart had very different delivery styles when talking about events at their company. Tina was more descriptive and emotional in her statements; Stuart was matter-of-fact. Business was just a game for him.

Although women and men have significant differences in their delivery styles, the delivery style doesn't necessarily alter the message content or intent. A man will make similar delivery choices whether he's talking about mowing the lawn or orchestrating a business merger. A woman will be fairly consistent whether she's discussing her children's eating habits or directing a hostile takeover. Pay attention to delivery styles as you interact at work and at home.

Avoiding gender stereotyping

What's wrong with these statements? "All men enjoy sports." "All women want children."

The problem is that not all men think or behave alike. Neither do all women. You can probably point to at least one person of the opposite gender with whom you have more in common than you do with some of the members of your own gender. A less-discussed problem is that men and women often stereotype members of their own gender. Dealing with people according to group membership is a tempting shortcut around getting to know them as individuals.

But at work, it's a shortcut full of pitfalls. An individual may have characteristics in common with your preconceived stereotype, but in the majority of cases, when you get to know someone, you'll find that he or she is far more complex and interesting than your stereotype.

Stereotyping is a standardized mental picture that is held in common by members of a group and that represents an oversimplified opinion, prejudiced attitude, or uncritical judgment. Unfortunately, stereotyping is a common form of prejudice. The three elements of gender stereotyping are:

- evaluating credibility according to gender,
- assessing an individual according to perceived gender group characteristics,
- making assumptions about someone's intentions because of gender.

Gender stereotyping is a serious handicap. Stereotyping causes you to believe something that may not be true. And taking action based on false information can lead to real problems.

Gender stereotyping
Credibility

Credibility is the belief that someone can do what he says he can. Men have credibility for leadership roles and are assumed to be the doers in an organization. Women have credibility as supporters and thinkers.

Character

People often assess others based on their gender group characteristics. Men are viewed as stronger, less sensitive, and more independent than women. Women are seen as weaker, more sensitive, and more dependent.

Intentions

"Boys want to be firemen and girls want to be mothers when they grow up." Those kinds of assumptions about intentions turn into "Men want to lead and have more responsibility" and "Women want supportive and creative roles."

Credibility stereotyping most often surfaces in business around leadership and support roles.

Roles

Leadership

We need a leader in that position. Facing the press for tough questioning isn't a woman's job. Let's ask Bryan.

Support

We need someone who understands people--probably a woman. Let's ask Helen if she'll take on the task.

Men and women are often assessed according to perceived gender group characteristics.

Characteristic

Strength

Statements such as "This is a man's job; it's tough" or "Women couldn't handle this" imply that women are weak and men are strong.

Sensitivity

Statements such as "This is a delicate situation; we need a woman's intuition" relate to the perception that men can't handle conversations that are emotionally charged.

Dependence

Statements such as "We need someone who can handle this on his own" or "It's a solo job" often imply that men are independent and women are not.

Making assumptions about intentions is a strong stereotype. Jack, a manager, talked with Susan, a new employee, about her career track.

Example

Jack

"I see you're in executive support. I imagine that'll be a good path for a few years. I assume you'll want to stay on that track until you have children."

Susan

"Well, actually, I intend to get into management over the next few years. I have two kids already and see no problem with being a parent and a manager."

Jack started by stereotyping Susan and assuming that a woman puts her family life ahead of her career. Susan had different intentions.

Intention stereotyping can also include assuming a man's or woman's interest in a co-worker of the opposite gender is socially or romantically motivated rather than professionally motivated. These kinds of assumptions can lead to concerns about sexual harassment and are seen as unacceptable.

These stereotypical views have a long history and go back countless generations from ancient hunter- gatherer societies through agricultural and industrial societies. But today's information-based society, with its new views on men and women, has led to a new world of stereotyping.

here are cues that indicate stereotyping is occurring. The cues involve the use of words that imply or directly state that a person conforms to one of the elements of gender stereotyping. Stereotyping is based on assumptions, not facts. Words such as "assume," "suppose," "believe," and "imagine" are all possible indicators of someone referring to her beliefs instead of reality. During your conversations, keep in mind the elements and views illustrated.

Rachel thought she was complimenting Mark, when actually, she was stereotyping him. Women and men can both stereotype the opposite gender without even being aware that they're doing it.

Once you start noticing when other people are making assumptions based on stereotypes, it becomes easier to identify when you're doing it and adjust your communication to relate to the individual rather than his or her gender.

Using the SAVE model

"The workplace war between men and women is one that may never be won--only slowly 'settled'--one problematic workday at a time." - Judith Tingley, founder and director of Performance Improvement Pros

There will always be two genders, and for the conceivable future, they'll have to work together. Ignoring differences in communication styles only perpetuates problems. The best solution in the workplace is for each gender to give a little. That means men and women need to incorporate the most effective communication elements of each gender. The SAVE model will help you keep talking with the opposite gender.

The SAVE model
Solve problems only when asked.

Women often talk to explore and understand. They are not seeking a fix or a solution every time they raise a question. Neither are men. The first element men and women should honor is to solve problems only when asked directly.

Address issues from a task-based perspective.

Men often do not want to explore the emotional side of a work issue. Women do not need to know everyone's psychological state to function at work. The second element both genders should honor is to address issues from a task-based perspective, not an emotional perspective.

Voice thoughts directly and concisely.

Many women have a habit of speaking vaguely in an effort to not sound harsh. But rambling, tentative statements confuse the listener about what you really need or want. The third element that both genders should use at work is to voice thoughts with direct, concise statements.

Employ open-ended questions.

As part of a competitive communication style, men resort to closed-ended questions that shut down communication. When you're on the same team, you want the best input. The fourth element that both genders should use at work is to employ open-ended questions.

Example - Gina was aware of the SAVE model and kept it in mind as she discussed a new project with Kurt, her manager. She used questions that helped Kurt provide additional depth on his insights. She also made sure she used clear, concise wording as she talked about the project plans. Gina avoided solving a resource problem Kurt mentioned but didn't ask her to fix. And although Kurt seemed agitated, Gina didn't ask him if something was wrong. At the end of the meeting, Kurt thanked Gina for her excellent work.

Adding flexibility to your communication style will not suddenly make you sound more "feminine" or "masculine," but it will improve your communication with the opposite gender.

By using the elements of the SAVE model, you can save yourself and others from some of the difficulties that can arise in intergender communication.

The "S" in SAVE stands for Solve problems only when asked. Have you ever tried to solve a problem for someone and then found that he didn't really want your help? If you think you hear a request for a solution but you're not sure, the easiest way to find out is to ask. For example, "Are you just exploring this issue, or would you like me to brainstorm a solution with you?" Solving problems when you're not asked can be viewed as controlling or just inappropriate.

Example - Steve and Patti were talking about hiring a new programmer. Patti mentioned she had a problem getting approval from human resources. Steve said he'd take care of the issue, but Patti replied that she was already working on it and could handle the job without his help, much to Steve's chagrin.

The "A" in SAVE stands for Address issues from a task-based perspective. It's possible to get your work done without understanding a co-worker's mood or feelings. Unless there's an obvious invitation or opening, it's best to address issues from a focus on tasks, not personalities.

Rita was working with Jake on an account plan. She noticed that he seemed angry. She asked if anything was wrong, and he replied: "It's personal. Let's just finish the plan." Rita felt humiliated by her own question.

The "V" in SAVE stands for Voice thoughts directly and concisely. By speaking concisely and in a direct manner, your listeners will know exactly what you're saying. You don't want to leave your listeners wondering.

Speaking style

Vague

"Do you think maybe you could have this in by this afternoon?" is vague and fuzzy and leaves the listener unsure of what to do.

Precise

"I need the report by 2:00 p.m." is clear and precise. There's no confusion or room for uncertainty.

How do you know whether you or someone else is using the SAVE model? The answer lies in how the conversation is going.

Example - see each part for more information on determining whether the SAVE model is being followed.

Solve problems only when asked.

Asking is the key to this element. If someone describes a problem or implies that there's a problem, don't offer a solution unless asked. If you do, you're not using this element of the SAVE model. Solving problems when not asked to will usually get you a negative response.

Address issues from a task-based perspective.

Don't ask questions that relate to someone's feelings or comment on how you think a

person feels. These are clear signals that you're not following this element of the SAVE model. Voice thoughts directly and concisely.

Using vague language leaves the listener uncertain and is a sign that you're missing this element of the SAVE model. Words such as "maybe," "possibly," "some," and "seemingly" don't really tell the listener exactly what you mean.

Employ open-ended questions.

If someone is asking either/or yes/no questions, then this element of the SAVE model is being missed. This can occur when someone wants to "be right" and control the conversation, which often stops after a question of this sort.

Lisa didn't follow the SAVE model and actually alienated her business partner. Taking the time to use the SAVE model could have helped Lisa and Scott have a more supportive and productive relationship.

The four elements of the SAVE model represent only a sampling of the ways you can be more flexible in your interactions with the opposite gender. You may think of more ideas on your own for being more flexible and "saving the day" in your own way.

- Solve problems only when asked.
- Address issues from a task-based perspective.
- Voice thoughts directly and concisely.
- Employ open-ended questions.

Learning aid - **Expectations**

List the names of male and female colleagues with whom you work closely and capture your thoughts on how you may stereotype them. Examine the areas of credibility, characteristics, and intentions as defined in the topic "Expectations."

Record the names of these colleagues and make a note of how you stereotype each of them.

Learning aid - Applying the SAVE model

List the names of people you converse with, rate how well you applied each element of the model (e.g. as poor, fair, or good), and then think about how you can do a better job of applying the model in the future. The elements of the SAVE Model to rate yourself on are:

- Solved problems only when asked
- Addressed issues from a task focus
- Voiced thoughts directly/concisely
- Employed open-ended questions

Record how you can do a better job of applying the SAVE model.

Unspoken Communication

A wink, a nod, a foot tapping, a raised eyebrow, a glance away...

Even though none of the listed actions involve words, they are all easily recognizable communications. Just as with verbal communication, there are a lot of differences in how men and women communicate nonverbally.

One person reclines, comfortably sprawled in a chair with legs splayed in front; the other person walks down the street taking hurried, petite steps and keeping arms still and close.

Which is the woman and which the man? Can you tell just by a description of the body language?

"Pay attention. I'm talking to you."

Men and women both agree with researchers that women are better listeners. Women tend to be active listeners who listen for the whole message. They listen for feelings and attitudes as well as words. Men are passive listeners who tend to listen superficially. They focus on the literal transcript.

Hemingway valued his listening skills. Those skills probably helped him in his remarkable career as a writer. Whatever your job, being successful at work usually depends on having the best information. A lot of information arrives in written form, but the vast majority of information is delivered orally, and most spoken information is delivered person to person. By becoming a more responsive listener, you'll have better information.

Understanding how nonverbal behavior contributes to communication

A wink, a nod, a foot tapping, a raised eyebrow, a glance away...

Even though none of the listed actions involve words, they are all easily recognizable communications. Just as with verbal communication, there are a lot of differences in how men and women communicate nonverbally.

One of the most significant variations between the genders is how they listen and what they hear. Listening is a behavior all its own, apart from other body language and nonverbal behavior.

The nonverbal behaviors of men and women affect intergender communication. In this lesson, you'll learn the value of understanding how nonverbal behavior contributes to communication:

- increased capacity to grasp the entire message,
- enhanced ability to respond appropriately,
- fewer misunderstandings.

Often what you don't say carries the most meaning, and it may be what others "hear" the loudest.

The three topics in this lesson will differentiate women's and men's nonverbal behavior and offer some techniques to help you improve your listening behavior. Men and women use different:

- body language,
- listening behavior,
- responsive listening techniques.

Nonverbal behavior and the associated gender

One person reclines, comfortably sprawled in a chair with legs splayed in front; the other person walks down the street taking hurried, petite steps and keeping arms still and close.

Which is the woman and which the man? Can you tell just by a description of the body language?

Men and women send different messages with their nonverbal behavior. Psychological research into business communication has determined that although 80 percent to 90 percent of meeting time is devoted to verbal discussion, only 20 percent or less of the actual message is conveyed by spoken words. At least 80 percent of the meaning is communicated by nonverbal elements.

Men and women have some significant differences in their nonverbal communication behaviors. These differences are:

• use of space

• physical orientation • touching.

The first difference between men and women is their use of space. Men generally require larger body zones than do women. Their use of space is relaxed, big, and open, and they use more wide, sweeping gestures. Women tend to compact themselves into a given space, seeing how petite they can make themselves.

Men stride, expanding into their space, whereas women walk in short, hurried steps. Men often stand with their feet apart. Women frequently keep their legs close together, one foot angled in front of the other like a ballet dancer.

Another difference in nonverbal communication styles between men and women is physical orientation. Physical orientation refers to how people stand when they're having a conversation.

Conversation type
Male conversation

Two men in conversation stand side by side, shoulders indirectly oriented, looking ahead rather than at each other. This positioning is more closed and less personal.

Female conversation

Women prefer establishing good rapport. They converse face-to-face so they can notice facial expressions, hand movement, and other nonverbal cues. This positioning is more open and more personal.

Besides physical orientation, men and women also use touch in different ways. Women use touch as a way of bonding and to build rapport. Men use touch more in a control context that conveys or expresses power.

Men

Initiating touch is a male power marker. A male boss might pat a shoulder as a greeting or initiate a high-five, but his subordinates would hesitate before patting him.

Women

Women are touched more in conversation by both men and women. People perceived as having less status are the more frequent recipients of touching.

Although many types of nonverbal behavior have been associated by researchers more with one gender than the other, you want to be careful not to stereotype automatically when you see certain behaviors.

The majority of what is communicated comes through nonverbal behavior. You can help avoid confusion and misunderstanding, especially in intergender communication, by becoming familiar with the differences between men's and women's preferred nonverbal communication styles. Men and women communicate differently in the way they use space, their physical orientation, and how they employ touch. Neither is right or wrong, just different.

Listening behaviors and the associated gender
"Pay attention. I'm talking to you."

Men and women both agree with researchers that women are better listeners. Women tend to be active listeners who listen for the whole message. They listen for feelings and attitudes as well as words. Men are passive listeners who tend to listen superficially. They focus on the literal transcript.

Listener Types
Active listeners
Women respond to the emotional as well as the literal message. This can confuse men.

Passive listeners
Men ignore the emotional content and usually respond only to the literal message. This can frustrate women.

Besides making good eye contact, women are also expressive with their faces. They nod and smile in encouragement while listening.

Besides glancing only at the speaker, men will mask their facial expressions when listening, giving few cues to their listening process.

Men's listening, like their speech, is goal-oriented. Women's listening, like their speech, is process- oriented.

Listening type

Goal-oriented

Men listen to hear if the message requires an action response from them. If the content

doesn't have a purpose, that is, if it doesn't require them to do something, they stop listening.

Process-oriented

Women notice the details of body language and facial expression which gives them insight into both the literal and emotional content. They listen to understand.

Simply knowing that men and women listen differently isn't enough. Both genders need to work at their listening behavior at work. Men need to increase their ability to hear the entire meaning of the message. Women need to decrease their perceived personalization of the message.

Listening techniques in an intergender work scenario

"I like to listen. I have learned a great deal from listening carefully. Most people never listen." - Ernest Hemingway

Hemingway valued his listening skills. Those skills probably helped him in his remarkable career as a writer. Whatever your job, being successful at work usually depends on having the best information. A lot of information arrives in written form, but the vast majority of information is delivered orally, and most spoken information is delivered person to person. By becoming a more responsive listener, you'll have better information.

Listening skills

Acknowledge the other person.

Acknowledging is a response that lets the speaker know you're fully there and listening.

Paraphrase the other person's statements.

Paraphrasing is restating the speaker's literal message in your own words. It lets the speaker know you're hearing the content of the message.

Reflect the emotion underlying the other person's statements.

Reflecting is stating the underlying emotional content of the speaker's message, or how the speaker feels. It lets the speaker know not only that you hear the message but also that you understand how the speaker feels about it.

If you pay attention the next time you have a conversation with someone you consider a good listener, you'll probably hear him or her using some or all of the responsive techniques that are standard tools used by good listeners.

Learning how to be a responsive listener will help you with your business and personal conversations.

Acknowledging consists of a simple verbal response that involves you interactively with the speaker. An acknowledgment is as simple as offering an "uh huh" or a "yes" to encourage the speaker to keep going, or asking a question related to what the speaker is saying.

Acknowledging outcomes

Encourage

Bo says, "This is a hard project." Your acknowledgement of "Yes, it is" can encourage him to continue what he's saying.

Clarify

Example - Joe says, "Tricia in marketing is such a moron." Your acknowledgment of "Did Tricia do something that upset you?" will help Joe clarify himself.

Paraphrasing consists of rephrasing the speaker's words. You repeat the content of the speaker's statement in different words--your words. By paraphrasing, you let the speaker know what you've heard, which gives you both a chance to make sure you're on the same track.

Example - Diane says, "Tricia makes too many personal calls and surfs the Internet all day." Your paraphrase of "Tricia is not getting her work done" lets your colleague know that you understand what she's saying.

Reflecting consists of acknowledging the feelings the speaker is expressing. By acknowledging someone's feelings, you help establish deeper levels of rapport.

Statement

A colleague says, "I always have more assignments than anybody else in this department."

Reflection

You say, "Sounds as if you're feeling overwhelmed." Notice that the reflection is about the emotion attached to the message, not the content of the message.

How do you know if you're being responsive in your listening? Primarily, you'll know by your counterpart's reactions. If she says you're not listening, then you're probably missing something in the communication. You just need to think before you respond. And if your counterpart sounds angry or sad, then reflecting that emotion may be the quickest way of establishing rapport.

Reflecting emotions

Acknowledge the other person.

Feedback other than questions or simple acknowledgments can cause the conversation to stop. If you take the conversation in a different direction, the speaker will not believe that you're listening. And negative feedback will stop a conversation completely.

Paraphrase the other person's statements.

Paraphrasing is restating what the speaker says in your own words. Changing topics is a clear signal that you're not listening to the speaker.

Reflect the emotion underlying the other person's statements.

Reflecting relates to the speaker's emotional state. Your reflection should refer to the feelings the speaker is experiencing. Referring to someone's sadness when he is angry is a poor reflection and will derail your conversation.

Using responsive listening techniques may feel artificial when you start, but you'll find them to be so effective that they will quickly become part of your habitual communication tool kit.

Women and men will always be different, and that's a wonderful thing. But when those differences interfere with clear communication, they hinder your ability to do your job. Because working relationships between men and women are now the norm for almost everyone in the work force, the most direct way to make those relationships more viable is to improve intergender communication.

Learning aid - Being a Responsive Listener

List the names of people you converse with and then rank your responsiveness under the following headings:

- acknowledged,
- paraphrased,
- reflected.

Then think about, and record, how you can be more responsive in the future.

CHAPTER FIVE

References & Glossary

References
1. *People Styles at Work: Making Bad Relationships Good and Good Relationships Better* - 1996, Bolton, Robert, and Dorthy G. Bolton
2. *Masters of Networking: Building Relationships for Your Pocketbook and Soul* - 2000, Miser, Ivan R., and Don Morgan, Bard Press,
3. *Cross Functional Teams* - 1997, Parker, Glenn M., Jossey-Bass,
4. *Reaching and Changing Frontline Employees* - Larkin, T.J., and Sandra Larkin, Harvard Business Review on Effective Communication, 1999
5. *Creative Meetings Through Power Sharing* - Prince, George M., Harvard Business Review on Effective Communication, 1999, Page(s) 59-78
6. *Customers As Partners: Building Relationships That Last* - 1994, Bell, Chip R., Berrett-Koehler Publishers

7. *Customer Once, Client Forever: 12 Tools for Building Lifetime Business Relationships* - 2001, Buckingham, Richard A., The Kiplinger Washington Editors Inc.

8. *The Value-Creating Consultant: How to Build and Sustain Lasting Client Relationships* - 2000, Carucci, Ron A., and Toby J. Tetenbaum

9. *Developing Knowledge-Based Client Relationships: The Future of Professional Services* - 2000, Dawson, Ross, Butterworth-Heinemann

10. *Trusted Partners: How Companies Build Mutual Trust and Win Together* - 1999, Lewis, Jordan D., The Free Press

11. *Customer Intimacy: Pick Your Partners, Shape Your Culture, Win Together* - 1996, Wiersema, Fred, Knowledge Exchange

12. *Multicultural Management* - 1998, Elashmawi, Farid, and Philip R. Harris, Gulf Publishing

13. *Communicating With Strangers* - 1992, Gudykunst, William B., and Young Yun Kim , McGraw-Hill

14. *Building Cross Cultural Competence* - 2000, Hampden-Turner, Charles M., and Fons Trompenaars, Yale University Press

15. *Diversity in the Workplace* - 1992, Jackson, Susan E., Guilford

16. *When Cultures Collide: Managing Successfully Across Cultures* - 1996, Lewis, Richard D., Nicholas Brealey Publishing

17. *Communicating in Organizations: A Cultural Approach* - 1995, Pepper, Gerald L., McGraw-Hill
18. *Cultural Issues in Business Communication* - 2000, Sellin, Robert, and Elaine Winters, Berkeley, CA: Program Facilitating and Consulting
19. *Culture Smart* - 1995, Thiederman, Sondra, Cross Cultural Communications
20. *He Says, She Says: Closing the Communication Gap Between the Sexes* - 1999, Glass, Lillian, Ph.D., Perigee
21. *Men Are From Mars, Women Are From Venus* - 1992, Gray, John, HarperCollins
22. *Talking from 9 to 5: Women and Men in the Workplace: Language, Sex and Power* - 1995, Tannen, Deborah, William Morrow
23. *Genderflex: Men and Women Speaking Each Other's Language at Work* - 1994, Tingley, Judith C.
24. *We're Just Good Friends: Women and Men in Nonromantic Relationships* - 1997, Werking, Kathy, The Guilford Press

Glossary

A

Adaptive communication - A technique for communication in which the speaker adapts his or her approach to meet the style and expectations of the listener.

Associational territory - Workplace territory that includes the contacts and personal associations one has.

C

Censure - Active disapproval or criticism.

D

Decisional territory - Workplace territory in which one has the authority to make decisions.

I

Informational territory - Workplace territory that is defined by the information or informational resources that one has in his or her possession.

Interfunctional - Describes a relationship or group that operates among various functions, departments, or divisions in an organization.

Interfunctional communications model - A model for improving interfunctional communications that consists of three parts: being respectful; acknowledging differences; and listening with an open mind.

V

Vestigial - Left over. Indicates a trace or sign of something that once existed but is no longer applicable and/or functioning. The genetic component of the human territorial instinct is vestigial.

www.ingramcontent.com/pod-product-compliance
Lightning Source LLC
Chambersburg PA
CBHW020904180526

45163CB00007B/2614